THE

FRIENDS OF CHRIST

IN THE NEW TESTAMENT:

THIRTEEN DISCOURSES,

BY

NEHEMIAH ADAMS, D. D.,

PASTOR OF THE ESSEX STREET CHURCH, BOSTON.

FIFTH EDITION.

BOSTON:
PUBLISHED BY JOHN P. JEWETT & CO.
CLEVELAND, OHIO:
JEWETT, PROCTOR, & WORTHINGTON.
NEW YORK: SHELDON, LAMPORT, & BLAKEMAN.
1855.

CORRESPONDENCE.

BOSTON, *April* 26, 1852.

REVEREND AND DEAR SIR: —

At a meeting of the members of your congregation, we have been appointed a committee to convey to you their earnest request that you will favor them, for publication, with a copy of the series of Sermons on "The Friends of Christ," which you have just closed.

We perform the duty assigned to us with great pleasure, and take leave to add to the wishes of the congregation our own, that those who heard the discourses may be indulged with an opportunity to peruse, thoughtfully and repeatedly, what they listened to with so much interest; and that those who did not hear them may be enabled to partake of their seasonable and important instructions.

We are, with sentiments of the highest regard and affection,

Your friends,

RUFUS CHOATE,
GEORGE ROGERS,
A. WILKINSON,
GEO. W. THAYER,
DAVID PIKE,
JOHN TAPPAN.

To REV. N. ADAMS, D. D.

BOSTON, *May* 4, 1852.

TO THE COMMITTEE OF THE ESSEX STREET CONGREGATION,

Dear Sirs: The request in your kind letter has induced me to think that the Sermons referred to, which were prepared in the ordinary course of ministerial labor, may be owned by Him whom they were intended to honor, as a means of further good. I therefore submit them to your disposal.

With great respect and affection,

Most truly yours,

N. ADAMS.

To Messrs. RUFUS CHOATE,
GEORGE ROGERS,
A. WILKINSON,
GEO. W. THAYER,
DAVID PIKE,
JOHN TAPPAN.

CONTENTS.

SERMON I.

THE WISE MEN FROM THE EAST.

MATTHEW II. 1, 2.

NOW WHEN JESUS WAS BORN IN BETHLEHEM, IN THE DAYS OF HEROD THE KING, BEHOLD, THERE CAME WISE MEN FROM THE EAST TO JERUSALEM, SAYING, WHERE IS HE THAT IS BORN KING OF THE JEWS? FOR WE HAVE SEEN HIS STAR IN THE EAST, AND ARE COME TO WORSHIP HIM.

OVER those mountains and wastes divided by the Tigris and Euphrates, a caravan shaped its way toward Jerusalem.

Departing from Persia, (according to the most approved opinion,) we see it winding its way over and around the steep, rough places of Kûrdistan, penetrating the fertile Assyrian plain, toiling through the parched places of Mesopotamia, and the deserts of Syria. It was a wearisome journey. Ezra, with a large company, and therefore travelling at a slow rate, was four months on his way from Persia to Jerusalem; so that probably not far from three months were occupied by this caravan in a journey of about fifteen hundred miles.

It was a company of Magi. They were the learned class among the people of the east, employed chiefly with the study of religion, medicine, and astronomy, including the superstitious observance and worship of the heavenly bodies, to which were assigned special influences over the destinies of men. The evening sky was to these Magi their book of revelation. Each orb and constellation had a certain character and certain influences ascribed to it; and in advising kings, in going forth with them to battle, and in directing the movements of armies, the Magi noted carefully what constellations and planets were in the ascendant. The nearness of one of the planets to the earth at the birth of a royal personage was used to foretell his character, and that of his reign.

For some time previous to the Saviour's birth, there was a wide-spread expectation among the nations, that a king was soon to be born who would rule the whole world. By means of the captivity of the Jews, their expectation of the Messiah, founded on the prophecies of their sacred books, was, of course, widely known; and these prophecies represented that Judea would be his birthplace, that he would be a benevolent king, bringing abundance of peace to the whole human race, the author of a golden age, unparalleled blessings from Heaven attending his reign, so that he became, long before his birth, according to the prediction of one of the Hebrew prophets, " the desire of all nations."

About the time of the Saviour's birth, it pleased God to publish the event in far distant Persia, by a method coinciding with the habits of the people in the east. Toward the west, the astrologers saw an unusual meteor; their books of science and their astronomical calculations had made no provision for such a sign, but, as the new king of the Jews was then expected, they hailed that strange orb as the announcement of his birth. We see the forbearance and kindness of God in thus falling in with the superstitions of these idolaters.

Had this star been one of the regular heavenly bodies, it is plain that no such unusual impression would have been made by it as was made by this new sign in the heavens. The evening star had always been seen in the west without exciting any special attention; the special brightness of a fixed star, for several nights in succession, would not have roused the Magi in so extraordinary a manner.

It is well known that the celebrated mathematician, Kepler, regarded the star of the wise men as the result of a conjunction between three heavenly bodies, such as occurred in the year of our Lord 1604, when Jupiter, Saturn, and Mars blended their rays, as he supposed; those planets being, at that time, in the sign of the Fishes, and a heavenly body then shed ding forth a strange and wonderful light in that quarter. Kepler calculated the conjunction of these planets as having taken place, with two of them, in the year of Rome 747, and with the three, in 748; in one of which years it is generally agreed that Christ was born. Some, who wish to reduce the number of miracles in the Bible, and the corresponding tax upon their faith, as low as possible, account in this manner for the star which the wise men saw. But even if the star had an orbit among the regular stars, its sudden appearance makes no great demand upon credulity, for He who "maketh peace in his high places" has, from the beginning, led forth, and has also taken away, heavenly bodies from the eyes of men.

An illustration of this is the celebrated star, first described by Tycho Brahe, which appeared on an evening of November, 1572, in the sign of Cassiopēia. It surpassed, in size and brilliancy, the planet Jupiter, and was visible sometimes at noon, which is never the case with any other planet but Venus. When other heavenly bodies were hidden by clouds, this new and strange orb was frequently seen through them. Its color was, at different times, white, yellow, red, gray, and leaden blue. In sixteen months from its first appearance it passed away, and has never since that time reappeared. This may serve to help the faith of some with regard to the appearance of a new and singular heavenly body at the birth of Christ. But there is the strongest reason to believe that the star which appeared to the wise men was not a fixed, nor a regular planetary, orb.*

God, who ordained it for a special purpose, disposed the minds of the Magi to fulfil that purpose, by creating among them an enthusiasm with regard to the wonderful sign in the west. Night after night, perhaps, they watched the stranger, till, at length, all doubt that it heralded a royal birth departed. It hung in the west toward Judea, the region where they had been expecting that a great king would soon appear; and their long-cherished interest in that event was greatly quickened by the special appointment, as it were, of a messenger which seemed to beckon them. They could not resist the divine call. No more would they watch the Pleiades, till they had followed after that new star. Arcturus and his sons might, for a season, measure their zone, the crooked Serpent sweep through his orbit, and the sworded Orion lie along the sky, unheeded, as to any prophetic signs in their spheres. The Star of Jacob was then in the ascendant, and filled the thoughts of the wise men; and so, impelled by an

* See "The Star of the Wise Men, being a Commentary on the second Chapter of Matthew, by Richard Chevenix Trench, B. D.;" to which valuable treatise I am greatly indebted in revising this Sermon for the press.

invisible hand, a company of them commenced a pilgrimage toward Jerusalem.

Interesting men! We love you as we follow your caravan in its dreary way along the beaten road or pathless wastes. None ever braved the desert for an object so great as that which excites your zeal.

The presence of a deputation of Magi from the east, in Jerusalem, asking, "Where is he that is born King of the Jews?" moved the whole city. No doubt the Magi expected to find Jerusalem excited with joy at the birth of the new king. "We have seen his star in the east, and are come to worship him;" to join with you in your joy, and bring you the congratulations of the eastern world.

Herod the Great was now in the thirty-fifth year of his reign. The appearance of a successor independently of him, of course, filled him with consternation; and whatever disturbed him, especially if it were the prospect of being supplanted, would fill Jerusalem with apprehensions of political disturbance, inasmuch as the Magi might prove to be the representatives of some combination in behalf of a new civil power.

So far was Herod from knowing that Christ was born, that he called the Jewish scribes, (for he was an Edomite,) and inquired of them what place their sacred books named as the Messiah's birthplace. It appears strange, perhaps, that, having ascertained this, he did not take secret measures to find and slay the infant, instead of waiting, as he proposed, for the Magi to return. For, though Herod was desperately wicked, all agree that he was a shrewd man, and of no common ability in the management of affairs. His shrewdness and tact are seen in this very transaction. He called the wise men privily, that his interest in the object of their mission might not be generally known. The only inquiry which he made of them was one which indicated no hostile purpose; while, bent as he was on finding and destroying the infant, he was employing the very best means to effect his object.

Had he sent forth messengers at once to find and slay the child, he could hardly hope to succeed, with nothing to point out which of the infants then in Bethlehem was the child sought, and with the risk, also, of giving alarm to the friends of the child in season to ensure its safety. Honorable men from the east, seeking the child "to worship him," would be far more likely to find him. "Go," said he, "and search diligently for the young child, and, when ye have found him, bring me word again, that I may come and worship him also." But this cunning and well-contrived arrangement, hiding a bloody purpose, enabled the wise men to fulfil the object for which God brought them from their far country.

And now the star which had beckoned them to

Judea, and which, perhaps, they did not expect to see any more after their entrance into Jerusalem, "came and stood over the place where the young child was." Words cannot express more intense feelings than the original of the passage which follows: "And when they saw the star, they joyed a great joy very much." The morning star of their hope had become the evening star of their desire accomplished. That lost guide, in confidence of whose truthful promise they had trod the desert, perhaps in conflict with many doubts, lest, after all, some meteor had only shone to bewilder and deceive them — behold, that kind friend, that faithful light-house, shines forth again, and, instead of tracking a way for them into far distant regions, it comes and rests very low, no higher, perhaps, than the smoke which curls from our chimneys, over the place where the young child was. They need not go from street to street, and from house to house, nor tax their patience, nor exercise their faith, any more. It was as though "Immanuel" were emblazoned on the door, or "King of kings and Lord of lords" were written on the wall.

The question whether this star were an orb of heaven, or a special sign created for this purpose, it would seem, must be removed, when we consider its position over the dwelling where the child was. It is plain that one of the regular heavenly bodies could not point to one dwelling more than to another.

From the three kinds of gifts which they presented, many have supposed that the number of the Magi was three. The Nestorian church generally taught that it was twelve. Three was the number ascribed to them in the prevailing traditions; names also being given to them, as, among others, Melchior, Gaspar, and Balthazar. They were held to be kings, representing the grand divisions of men—Melchior being put for Shem, Gaspar for Ham, and Balthazar for Japhet. This explains the Ethiopian complexion given to one of them in the pictures of the "Adoration." The passages which are so uniformly regarded as being fulfilled by them, "And the Gentiles shall come to thy light, and kings to the brightness of thy rising," (Isa. lx. 3,) and "The kings of Tarshish and of the isles shall bring presents, the kings of Sheba and Seba shall offer gifts," (Ps. lxxii. 10,) have given rise to the belief that they were kings, and accordingly the Feast of Epiphany was, in the middle ages, most commonly called the Feast of the Three Kings. The literature which has been connected with this brief account by Matthew, of the wise men, is hardly exceeded in variety by that of any other part of the New Testament. Cologne, upon the Rhine, the "City of the Three Kings," claims to possess their relics, and has given them a splendid shrine.* But it is needless to say that all this lore is probably the fruit of the imagination. If they were only sheiks, or emîrs, the word "kings," in the prophetic passages just quoted, would be proper. Whether the apostle Thomas baptized them, and whether they helped him to evangelize India, and whether they died as martyrs, or what became of them upon their return from Judea, are questions upon which the Bible gives us no information. But the brief, inspired record respecting them is full of interest and instruction.

I. THE COMING OF THE WISE MEN TO THE INFANT JESUS WAS AN ACT OF ADORATION.

The word rendered "worshipped," in the passage which speaks of the prostration of the wise men, it is said, does not necessarily imply any thing more than an act of respectful salutation, the same word being used in speaking of acts of courtesy between man and man.

But as Peter refused to receive the worship expressed by this same word, from Cornelius, saying, "I myself also am a man," and as the angel said to the evangelist John, who fell down before him, with the same worship, "See thou do it not; worship God," we cannot conclude, from the word itself, that

* See a most interesting article on the Cathedral at Cologne, in the London Quarterly Review, vol. lxxviii., 1846.

adoration was not intended by the wise men. Let us look, then, at the probabilities of the case.

Had the wise men regarded the Messiah merely as an earthly king, it would have been a most contemptuous and daring act to have proclaimed in Herod's dominions, nay, in the metropolis itself, "We have come to worship him." This would not be an act of "wise men." While they called the Messiah "King of the Jews," they must have regarded him as having a kingdom which did not conflict with that of Herod, of a heavenly nature, warranting, as the birth of an heir to no earthly kingdom would warrant, such a journey, and such respect as theirs

Here let it be considered, that the wise men may not have known, to its full extent, the intention of an overruling Providence in their coming to the feet of Christ; nor may they have understood their enthusiasm, with regard to this new-born personage, which brought them so far. Their habits and customs as astrologers made this act natural to them, while they may have been, and we believe that they were, like the prophets, under the excitement of inspiration, who did not fully know the vast import of many of their predictions.

We cannot believe — indeed, it is too great a tax on our credulity to ask us to believe — that God appointed this miraculous star to bring those sages from their distant land merely to pay their respects to a remarkable child. There is an air about the narrative which conveys something more to the mind than this. Self-interest did not prompt them. They had no favors to ask or expect of that child; they would be dead or far away when he should be old enough to ascend a throne; but they laded their camels with gifts for him evidently from a disinterested desire to pay some homage to him. What, then, was the nature of that homage?

Let us read this narrative, and learn to read the Bible in the same way, not with the unbeliever's eyes and heart, but with our own eyes, and our own believing hearts. It is one of the pernicious effects of sceptical opinions, that we subject the Bible in our own thoughts, even when we read it for devotional purposes, to the criticisms made by unbelievers; we are injuriously affected by the doubts and cavils of others. These may help us to examine narrowly the evidences of our faith, but let them not have the effect upon us, if we can help it, to make our faith timid. As those who honor the Son even as they honor the Father; as those who need not still to be laying the foundations of their faith in the Saviour; as those who have learned to say to him, My Lord and my God, let us contemplate this coming of the wise men to Christ, and see if there be not every probability of its being intended by the divine Spirit as an act of adoration.

That young child, then, whom we see in his mother's arms, while Persian wise men fall before him on the humble floor, who is he? whom do we believe him to be? It is he of whom we read, "In the beginning was the Word, and the Word was with God, and the Word was God." It is the great "mystery of godliness, God manifest in the flesh." It is he who afterward stilled the tempest, opened the eyes of the blind, raised the dead. It is he who came to put away sin by the sacrifice of himself; "the Lamb of God, which taketh away the sin of the world." It is he before whom the heavenly hosts were afterward seen prostrate, crying, "Worthy is the Lamb that was slain to receive power, and riches, and wisdom, and strength, and honor, and glory, and blessing." That scene between the wise men and the child Jesus is more than a mere act of respect to a remarkable infant. In their imperfect state of knowledge, as was just before observed, these wise men probably did not know the full extent and meaning of their worship. We, to whom Christ is more fully revealed, can see in that prostration of the wise men an act of religious devotion intended by the divine Spirit, though the wise men may not fully have comprehended the meaning of their own act. Our souls join with those Gentiles to worship that babe who was God manifest in the flesh, having then those attributes of Deity which he will have when he comes in his glory and all his holy angels with him, and before him are gathered all nations.

While many see nothing in the visit of the wise men to Christ but superstition, oriental reverence for royalty, and the zeal of courtly men to find or make occasion for acts of condescending respect, he who sees dwelling in Christ all the fulness of the Godhead bodily will not ask the lexicographer nor the unregenerate commentator whether the passage imports real worship. "When he bringeth in his first begotten into the world, he saith, Let all the angels of God worship him." He who believes that by the Son all things were created that are in heaven or in earth, visible and invisible, whether they be thrones, or dominions, or principalities, or powers, has no question what worship the angels, his creatures, paid him, when he assumed man's nature.

It may truly be said that a large part of the "comfort of the Scriptures," as the apostle expresses it, to a pious heart, is derived from comparing spiritual things with spiritual, from the confirmatory influence of the several parts of the Bible in their relation to each other, and from the discovery of probable allusions and intended coincidences, as well as from the more explicit fulfilment of types and prophecies, and truths directly asserted. Over this source of spiritual enjoyment in reading the Bible a sound discretion should, of course, preside.

Believing, then, that the babe at Bethlehem was Immanuel, God with us, we believe that the visit of the wise men was intended by the divine Spirit to be an act of adoration in honor of the incarnate Word, and also for the comfort and encouragement of all who at that time were waiting for the Messiah. As a choir may sing a piece which some more spiritual and devout hearers will enjoy far more than they, and adopt it as their own offering of praise to God, so this act of the wise men, no doubt, was received and seconded, by many a pious heart in Jerusalem and elsewhere, as a sacrifice to the Saviour. Many a heart that had waited long for the consolation of Israel, would see in the coming of the wise men a strong confirmation of their faith and hope. In that Jerusalem which is said to be "troubled" at the arrival of these men from the east, there was a hidden Israel, the Simeons and Annas, who did not share in the consternation of the king and the unbelieving world. God visited this his chosen people in the coming of the wise men, and gave them a glimpse of the way in which the prophetic Psalms and the visions of Isaiah and of the minor prophets would be fulfilled. God will not leave his people comfortless who wait for him. Were nothing else effected by the visit of the wise men, this warranted their mission, that their coming fulfilled the hopes of the devout men and women who were longing and waiting for the promised Saviour.

Nor did the friends and worshippers of Christ at that day alone receive comfort and joy from the act of the wise men. All of every age who love him and espouse his cause, and are praying and waiting for his final triumph in the earth, may see in this adoration by the wise men a prophecy and illustration of the future glory of Christ, when he shall be King of nations as he is now King of saints. "The kings of Tarshish and of the isles shall bring presents: the kings of Sheba and Seba shall offer gifts. Yea, all kings shall fall down before him: all nations shall serve him." Ps. lxxii. 10, 11. This act of the wise men we adopt as ours, the future homage of the nations we make our own, and our personal gratitude and thanksgiving take the form of earnest prayer that the Saviour may soon receive the love and adoration of all the earth. The cause of foreign missions rises in majesty and beauty, and affords us ways in which to express, by the consecration of ourselves and our children to Christ, our love and thankfulness, while our full hearts find relief in those assemblies for prayer and praise which have regard to the universal extension of the Redeemer's conquests in the earth.

II. The history of the wise men is an instance of the increase and the rewards of earnest faith.

Though we may need nothing to persuade us of the power of God to fulfil those promises which relate to the conversion of the world, yet when we see the eastern world aroused by a meteor, and turning their eyes to the birthplace of Christ, we are furnished with an illustration of the infinite ease with which God can and will, in the fulness of time, make nation after nation bow to the sceptre of the Redeemer. By some events of Providence, no less interesting in their kind than the appearance of the star to the Persian sages, and falling in with the habits or circumstances of the different nations as that star coincided with the thoughts and pursuits of the Magi, revolutions of popular opinion will occur which will fulfil the prediction, A nation shall be born in a day. Happy will those missionaries, and ministers, and christians be, who, with long patience, shall be found laboring and praying for those days, and shall have their faith rewarded, when, by the great outpouring of his Spirit, the Lord, whom they seek, shall suddenly come to his temple.

Not merely to the Simeons and Annas of Jerusalem, nor to those who already love and worship him, but to every soul for whom Christ came to be a Saviour, does this act of the wise men speak encouragement. The object of these discourses is, to present the Saviour as an object of faith, and love, and worship; to excite those feelings which sinners should have to their Saviour; and if any are ashamed of Christ, to show them in what ways some of our fellow-men, from every rank and in every condition, have expressed their love and worship; and to make it appear that all things are but loss compared with the excellency of the knowledge of Christ Jesus our Lord. Perhaps Christ, as a sacrifice for sin, is beyond the present measure of your faith. He is the great mystery of godliness, which, because you cannot fathom it, you do not receive; and, as Judge of the living and the dead, perhaps he awakens your fears.

Begin, then, where the wise men began, supposing your knowledge and your belief to be even as limited as theirs; but, adopting their desire and zeal to know something more of Christ, like them, 'follow on to know the Lord.' Let us trace the progress of their faith.

The star shone at a great distance, but in the direction of Judea; and these wise men arose and followed it. But when they had entered on their way, the star, for a large part of the time, if not entirely, must have disappeared. In the daytime, of course, they could not see it; in stormy and dark nights it was veiled; and thus, through their long and wearisome journey, they must, to a great degree, have walked by faith.

Not supposing that a king could be born out of the metropolis, they bent their way toward Jerusalem, inquiring for Christ. Instead of finding the great city moved with joy at his birth, it would seem as though the city had the first information of it from these Persians. The story of the shepherds, perhaps, had been treated with ridicule, and was forgotten; and the arrival of the Magi, with such an inquiry, only had the effect to trouble the king, and the whole city with him. Nothing daunted by this, nothing chilled in their faith and zeal, they literally followed on to know the Lord, seeking him with all the heart; and, pursuing their way to humble Bethlehem, behold, the star which they saw in the east came and stood over the place where the young child was.

If we were half as zealous to know the truth respecting Christ, and the way of salvation by him, as these heathen were to find him, all our wishes would be crowned with complete success. We are strongly disposed to hope and to believe that they were not moved to perform such a journey, and such an act of love and worship, to die, after all, without a saving knowledge of the Redeemer. Supposing them to have become acquainted with the gospel, they must have reflected with great satisfaction on the pains they took to find the Saviour, the faith they exercised, their perseverance, and, finally, their not being offended at the lowly condition in which they found him, though their imaginations had, no doubt, presented him to their minds in a manner corresponding with the sublime sign which had distinguished his birth. If they took with them to their home the sacred books of the Jews; if devout men had been moved, during their brief sojourn in the neighborhood of Jerusalem, to disclose to them such thoughts and feelings, concerning Jesus, as Zacharias, and Elizabeth, and Simeon, and others like them entertained; if, along their homeward journey, by day and by night, they read, and prayed, and talked concerning the Messiah, and found that they could worship still at the feet of that every where present Saviour, in the desert, and in Persia, as well as in Bethlehem; and if, returning to their people with this song in their hearts and upon their lips, "For unto us a child is born, unto us a son is given, and his name shall be called Wonderful, Counsellor, the Mighty God, the Everlasting Father, the Prince of Peace," they thus became the worshippers of the true God and the Redeemer, what gain must they have felt that their long and dreary journey had brought them; what caravan ever brought back treasures to be compared with those unsearchable riches of Christ, of which they had become possessed;

and what must have been their joy as they turned, from worshipping the host of heaven, 'to serve the living and true God, and to wait for his Son from heaven, even Jesus, which delivered us from the wrath to come.'

No distant, silent star beckons us, like them, to seek Christ. We have a more sure word of prophecy — a Bible, in which prophets and apostles conspire to bring us to the Saviour; his history is finished; we have not only his manger, but his cross, his tomb. Judea, Samaria, Galilee are imprinted with his familiar footsteps; his resurrection and ascension, the gift of the Holy Ghost, the testimony and blood of martyrs, the conversion of souls already without number, all perform that office for us which that solitary star rendered to these wise men. But faith is not in proportion to the amount of evidence. 'Prophets teach the Jews in vain; a silent star beckons the Gentiles; they arise and follow.' Still, the same promise assures us of success, if we follow after the small portion of light which our unbelieving eyes take in; still, he that seeketh findeth, if he seeks, like these wise men, with all the heart.

These wise men will, hereafter, condemn those nations who, on the first news of Christ, and salvation by him, should have received the gospel, but still reject it. The Queen of Sheba, it seems, is summoned as a witness, at the last judgment, against the men of the Saviour's time; for she came from the utmost parts of the earth to hear the wisdom of Solomon, while a greater than Solomon was with the unbelieving men of that age. So if we, with all our knowledge of Christ, should fail to believe on him, the sight of that company of wise men from the east, appearing, in the last judgment, before the Saviour, to be openly acknowledged by him, as a consequence of their faith and zeal, would powerfully condemn our indolence and unbelief, and leave us without excuse. Could we then return to earth, no pilgrimages, sufferings, zeal, and love would seem too much for so great an object as a personal interest in the work of redemption. Yet this is offered to us every Sabbath, and as often as we open the Scriptures. With the example of the wise men before us, and all that serves to illustrate and enforce the privilege and duty of believing on Christ, with every opportunity to obtain all that others have been obliged to purchase at vast expense, let us be sure that we be not thrust down from such exalted privileges to a deeper hell. It is not enough to commend religion by approving its doctrines and its influence. "He that believeth not is condemned already, because he hath not believed in the name of the only-begotten Son of God."

If those wise men are now among the redeemed, having washed their robes and made them white in the blood of the Lamb, what thoughts and feelings they must have, as they recollect the star in its first appearance to them; the difficulties which they overcame in following after it; the joy they felt when it reappeared, and gave a divine seal of approbation to their effort; their first sight of the infant Jesus; the impressions made upon them when, in this young mysterious potentate, as they believed him to be, they found the King of kings and Lord of lords! As they cast their crowns at his feet, they remember the gold, and frankincense, and myrrh which they once brought so far and laid there; they adore the sovereign love which selected them in their idolatrous land, and brought them to worship at those feet, and now rewards their gifts and their zeal, which were themselves the work of divine grace, with heavenly blessings. Among the happy spirits in heaven, these wise men must have no common joy in thinking of the method by which they were brought to the knowledge of Christ, and their salvation was secured. Who, of all the armies of heaven, fall at the feet of Christ with more affecting recollections, or with greater reason for gratitude and praise? Of the innumerable friends of Christ in heaven, who more suitably lead the Gentile church than those who were the first fruits of his advent, the trophies of victories won by him while yet in his manger at Bethlehem? And yet every one of us who shall be saved will be an instance and illustration of sovereign mercy; and in proportion to the strength of our faith and love shall we be happy in the recollections of earth, in the society of just men made perfect, and be qualified for future employment in the service of God.

We read no more of these wise men but that they returned to their own country. They carried with them, of course, the news of the Saviour, and no doubt were instrumental in advancing the new religion in the east. Were we allowed to indulge our fancy, as the Christian writers of the middle ages have done, and embellish the history of these wise men with imaginary incidents, we might do it, perhaps, after this manner. Persia, we would say, has not yet ceased to feel the benefit, indirectly, of their early homage at the feet of the infant Saviour. We cannot fail to remember, in connection with these Magi, that to their fellow-countrymen, the Nestorians of Persia, we are now sending the means of reëstablishing among them a pure Christianity. That people are remarkable from early times for their substantial orthodoxy. Nestorius was excommunicated by the Papal church for denying that Mary was the mother of God, and refusing to worship her; and it is interesting to notice here that the wise men paid no homage to Mary. A peculiar tone of piety characterizes the Nestorian converts, and it may be that they are blessed, and that great blessings are yet in ıeserve for them, in consequence of the zealous efforts of the Magi to find Christ. For God is a rewarder of them that diligently seek him, and he remembers mercy to a thousand generations.*

* Extract from the memoir of Mrs. Judith S. Grant, late missionary to Persia, pp. 176–178: —

"The place of her sepulture is within the outer enclosure or court of a Christian church, where, for many centuries, the lamp of truth, if not of vital piety, has been kept burning, though with a dim and flickering light. It is the Church of Mary, the mother of Jesus; and you may be interested to learn the tradition of the Nestorians regarding its history. They are confident of the truth of the general belief that Oroomiah was the residence of the renowned Zoroaster, the reformer of that primitive system of idolatry which found a God in the sun, moon, and stars, and the unextinguished fires on their holy altars. Zoroaster, say the Nestorians, was a disciple of Jeremiah, and having learned from him the promised advent of the Messiah, he taught it to his followers, assuring them that, directed by his star, they would be the first to pay him reverence.

As their tradition is remarkably corroborated by Abulpharagius, I will quote his language: "Zeradusht (Zoroaster,) the preceptor of the Magi, taught the Persians concerning the manifestations of Christ, and ordered them to bring gifts to him in token of their reverence and submission. He declared that in the latter days a pure virgin should conceive, and that as soon as the child was born a star would appear, blazing, even at noonday, with undiminished lustre. 'You, my sons,' exclaimed the venerable seer, 'will perceive its rising before any other nation. As soon, therefore, as you shall see the star, follow it whithersoever it shall lead you, and adore the mysterious child — offering your gifts to him with the profoundest humility. He is the Almighty WORD, which created the heavens.' 'It came to pass,' say the Nestorians, 'as Zoroaster predicted. The Magi ("wise men") of Persia were the first to discover the promised star; and, in obedience to their prophet, they hastened to pay their devotions to the new-born King. They took with them gold as a suitable present, if he were an earthly king; but as they had been apprised of his celestial character, they also brought frankincense and myrrh, which they were accustomed to burn as a perfume in their religious adoration.' On their return to the native abode of their prophet at Oroomiah, they brought with them some of the swaddling clothes of the incarnate Divinity, which were subsequently used as a sacred relic in consecrating the first Christian church of this land, which they named in honor of the blessed mother Mary, (Nana Mariam.)"

We have named the Wise men from the East, 'Friends of Christ,' and have given them a prominent place among that honorable number whom we are to consider in these discourses under that name. It is encouraging to notice how little of true faith in Christ, and what imperfect knowledge of him, they probably had when they came to his feet. And yet what consequences have flowed to them in their usefulness, during their lives, in directing the attention of others to Christ, in comforting the mourning people of God, in giving an example of zeal and faith to those who have more knowledge of Christ than they. This teaches us that with whatever motive we seek Christ, or however imperfect and deficient our knowledge of him, we cannot seek in vain, nor will our sincere efforts to know him better fail to be rewarded. "A bruised reed he will not break; and smoking flax he will not quench."

It deserves a passing notice, in conclusion, that

III. The adoration of the Magi affords a remarkable illustration of our Saviour's humility and meekness.

We cannot suppose that the knowledge of this adoration was withheld from him when he came to years of understanding. What effect might we suppose it would have had on any one of us, had he been told that, when he was an infant, learned men came in a company and did him reverence; that wise men from the continent of Europe made a pilgrimage to his feet? But the Saviour was subject to his parents, and worked at his trade as a carpenter. When he began his public ministry, and selected his first apostles, did he choose Magi for his ministers? No, but Andrew, and Peter, and Philip, and Bartholomew, and the sons of Zebedee. With what truthfulness and beauty, then, does that gracious invitation to each of us proceed from his lips: "Come unto me, all ye that labor and are heavy laden, and I will give you rest. Take my yoke upon you, and learn of me, for I am meek and lowly in heart, and ye shall find rest to your souls." There is only one instance in the New Testament in which the Man of Sorrows is said to have rejoiced; and this was in connection with the truth that God had hid the things of his kingdom from the "wise and prudent," and had "revealed them unto babes." It gratified the benevolence of Christ to think that the humble, unlettered poor of our race were specially the objects of divine compassion, while those who were wise in their own conceit, in consequence of their human learning or gifts, were passed by. When the Saviour, who had had the wise men of the east at his feet, stretches forth his hand, and says, Blessed are ye poor, for yours is the kingdom of God, he excites the confidence and joy of every one whom he honors with being his ambassador, and he should draw all men unto him.

The title, 'Friends of Christ,' naturally leads to the inquiry, Am I a friend of Christ? Perhaps every one will readily answer, Yes. Mention some proof of it. Take time, and see if you are a friend of Christ by any such proof as commonly evinces friendship. How much do you pray to Christ? what communion have you with him? how often do you repeat with yourself his precious name? on whom of his disciples have you ever bestowed a gift, a kind word or look, for the reason, and for that reason only, that you believed him to be a friend of Christ? what have you ever done for that cause which is all in this world that Christ holds dear?

It is a truth to which every minister of Christ testifies from personal experience, that every thing which man can do to influence his fellow-men is easier than to make them love Him who is "the chiefest among ten thousand," and "altogether lovely." Amid unsuccessful efforts for this object, saying, Who hath believed our report? and mourning that we can persuade so few to love and honor the Saviour, it is always refreshing and encouraging to look into the New Testament and contemplate the instances of love to Christ as there recorded. It reassures us of the Saviour's infinite excellence; it shows us how the human heart has responded to his claims upon its love and homage, while the prophecies and promises of the Bible come to our aid, showing that He, whom, having not seen, we love, shall yet be loved and adored on earth and in every land, and by myriads of our race in heaven.

This series of discourses on the Friends of Christ in the New Testament, is begun, therefore, with the view and in the hope of assisting every one, by example, to love and honor the Saviour of the world, to become his friend, and to secure the friendship of Him whose loving kindness is better than life. You will find the question constantly recurring, Are you a friend of Christ? The answer to this question will, at the great harvest of the earth, determine whether the reaping angels shall place us with the wheat or with the tares. The Judge himself will assign, as the reason for the sentence which he will pronounce upon us, the evidence which our present lives afforded whether we were, or were not, his friends.

SERMON II.

SIMEON.

LUKE II. 25, 26.

AND BEHOLD, THERE WAS A MAN IN JERUSALEM, WHOSE NAME WAS SIMEON; AND THE SAME MAN WAS JUST AND DEVOUT, WAITING FOR THE CONSOLATION OF ISRAEL; AND THE HOLY GHOST WAS UPON HIM. AND IT WAS REVEALED UNTO HIM BY THE HOLY GHOST THAT HE SHOULD NOT SEE DEATH BEFORE HE HAD SEEN THE LORD'S CHRIST.

THOUGH the world that was made by Him knew Him not, there were those who, by the Spirit of God, were moved to honor and welcome the Redeemer, at his entrance upon earth.

One of the first that we read of was an aged man, distinguished for the uprightness and piety of his life, by the name of Simeon. It is nowhere asserted that he was an old man, but when we find that a passage of Scripture, and especially a narrative, has made a certain impression, we should be slow to call it in question; for we may suppose that the Bible has had, among its millions of readers, minds as shrewd and critical as any at the present day.

Though the old age of Simeon is nowhere asserted, it may be easily inferred from the brief account of him before us. It was revealed to him by the Holy Ghost that he should not see death till he had seen the Lord's Christ. This makes the impression that, in the course of nature, he had reason to be expecting death, and that a special exemption from it had been assured to him until he should see Christ; so that, when he saw him, he regarded it as the sign of his speedy departure from the world, which he would not have done had there not been reason, in his condition, to feel that his continuance in life was not long to be expected.

We may, therefore, regard him as an old man, and full of days, with those infirmities and sorrows which are peculiar to advanced years; and yet, in the midst of them, there was an earnest hope and expectation to see that promised Lord, and this desire was like a staff to him while he daily waited for the tidings of the Saviour's birth, which his own great age, and the near approach of death, in the natural order of things, convinced him could not be far off.

He was "a just man," of blameless life, "a devout man," living under the influence of religious contemplations, and performing his duties to God, in public and private, with sincerity and in an exemplary manner.

He "waited for the consolation of Israel." The prophets had spoken of the Saviour's birth as an event that would bring great consolation with it to the hearts of all who loved God. Thus Isaiah, predicting the coming Messiah, said, "Comfort ye, comfort ye my people, saith your God." "Sing, O heavens, and be joyful, O earth, for the Lord hath comforted his people." "As one whom his mother comforteth, so will I comfort you, and ye shall be comforted in Jerusalem." Jeremiah, the weeping prophet, had spoken in the same manner, and Zechariah, so near to the time of Christ, had said, "For the Lord shall yet comfort Zion, and shall yet choose Jerusalem." The modern Jews speak of the days of the Messiah, whom they still expect, as the days of consolation, and a form of oath among them is this: "I swear by my desire of seeing the consolation." When we call to mind how kings and prophets had desired to see the times of Christ, but died without the sight, how the glowing rhapsodies of Isaiah, and the revelations made to Daniel, with regard to Messiah's kingdom, had excited the national mind, while those who had correct spiritual views of the Redeemer had associated him with the forgiveness of sins, through faith in the blood which was to abolish the ceremonial law, and speak that peace to the guilty conscience which types and forms could do only by a borrowed power, we can easily suppose that the desire to see Christ was a most intense desire, combining all the patriotic feeling, and the love of liberty, and the hope of deliverance from the Roman power; and also in some, like Simeon, the more spiritual expectation of coming nearer to God than by the help of altars and slain beasts; as the prophet had said: "But he is wounded for our transgressions, he is bruised for our iniquities; the chastisement of our peace is upon him, and with his stripes we are healed." To see that which Abraham, their great ancestor, desired to see, and of which, by faith, he had a distinct idea presented to his mind, and was glad; to see him whom great Aaron typified, but before whom Aaron must resign his mitre and his breastplate; to look on him that was greater than Moses, bringing grace and truth instead of a broken and fiery law; to see him who was David's Lord, and yet David's son,—this expectation surpassed all that we can imagine, and, as the time drew near, the desire must have risen to intensity.

This aged Simeon feared that he should close his eyes in death before that day should dawn and that daystar arise in his heart. How we sometimes long to live that we may behold certain things which, if we are in heaven, we shall enjoy as fully, and, indeed, more perfectly, than here. And yet we feel that to see those things in our day, among the living, to share in the joy of others in beholding the fulfil ment of a promise or hope, will comfort our last hours, gently break our hold on life, and make us more willing to die. God had graciously condescended to grant the desires of Simeon in this particular, and the time drew near.

One day he "came by the Spirit into the temple," moved by a divine impulse to repair to the house of God, no doubt to perform his devotions. God had ordered it that, at that moment, the parents of Jesus should bring him in for the rite of circumcision. There the disclosure was made to this aged man that his desire was fulfilled: 'The Lord whom ye seek' has 'suddenly come to his temple; even the messenger of the covenant whom ye delight in, behold, he is come, saith the Lord of hosts.'

No doubt some divine communication was made to the mind of Simeon at that time; for we are told that the Holy Ghost was upon him, so that he was inspired to know who the child was, and to utter the predictions which followed. "Then took he him up in his arms, and blessed God."

See now the heart of the old man, long buffeting with infirmity and the signs of approaching dissolution. He speaks, first of all, concerning the laying down of the load of life, with that desire gratified which alone had made life tolerable. "Lord," he says, "now lettest thou thy servant depart in peace, according to thy word; for mine eyes have seen thy salvation." Come, death, so long waiting for me; I have nothing more to live for; my hopes and wishes are fulfilled, for I have seen the Lord's Christ. I leave the world with the Messiah born into it. My people, my kindred, ye Gentile nations, your Saviour has come. Farewell.

The act of the venerable old man in the temple, evidently under the influence of a prophetic spirit, must, of course, have astonished the parents of Christ. "And Joseph and his mother marvelled at those things which were spoken of him." Mine eyes, he said, have seen thy salvation, which thou hast prepared before the face of all people; a light to lighten the Gentiles, and the glory of thy people Israel. To the simple, humble parents of the child, these solemn words, and, no doubt, the most impressive and affecting appearance of the old man, holding the child in his arms, and pouring out utterances of prophetic ecstasy, were more than they could comprehend, notwithstanding the wonders attending his conception and birth. But, to their marvel, the holy seer replied with other words no less surprising. "And Simeon blessed them, and said unto Mary his mother," (how much nature there is in speaking to the mother about the child, rather than to the father,) "Behold, this child is set for the fall and rising again of many in Israel, and for a sign that shall be spoken against; (yea, a sword shall pierce through thine own soul also;) that the thoughts of many hearts may be revealed."

The brief history of this aged worshipper of the child Jesus, as well as his words of significant import, furnish much instruction. The object of these discourses, as already stated, is to illustrate the faith and love of which Christ has been the object, and thereby to encourage and quicken our faith and love, and, if need be, to remove the coldness of our affections.

I. Simeon is an example to us of faith in Christ, and of strong affection towards him.

Is this the promised Messiah, this babe in the arms of a poor woman of Bethlehem, her husband bearing in his basket "a pair of turtle doves or two young pigeons," unable to bring the usual offering of a lamb, but availing himself of the alternative offering prescribed for the poor? What a sight is this! What an entrance into the world, if this be the Messiah! Does this meet and fulfil Isaiah's vision, "For unto us a child is born, unto us a son is given, and his name shall be called Wonderful, Counsellor, the Mighty God, the Everlasting Father, the Prince of Peace"? Is this "the desire of nations," "the Lord whom ye seek," "even the messenger of the covenant"? Is this "the King of the Jews," this "the man that is my fellow, saith the

Lord of hosts"? What faith Simeon must have had, to believe the simple word of God in the face of all the disparaging and contradictory circumstances of that child.

But perhaps we are tempted to say, No wonder that he believed, notwithstanding all these unfavorable circumstances; for he was moved by the Holy Ghost, and so was led, by a secret impulse upon his mind, to feel that that child was the Messiah.

And is it so easy to believe under strong impressions, when every thing that is circumstantial discourages faith? How is it with us? We have a persuasion that certain doctrines are taught in Scripture, but there is opposition to them. Some treat them with scorn, and, what is worse, we cannot explain the mysteries in them, and must confess that they are above reason. Do we still embrace the truth, as Simeon did the child Jesus, and say, Mine eyes have seen thy salvation?

We have a strong persuasion, confirmed by observation, that we ought, without delay, to make our peace with God. By impressions upon our minds, as strong as can be made consistently with our freedom, the Holy Ghost says, "To-day, after so long a time, if ye will hear his voice, harden not your hearts." But our companions entice us, the world charms us, pleasure sings with enchanting voice, alluring us to fancied future joys, which we feel we must obtain before we give our hearts to God, and procrastination promises a future time for repentance; and so we pass, heedless, by opening graves and alarming providences, and stop our ears against conscience and the Bible, and put our souls in jeopardy for that endless duration after death. Is it easy to obey strong impulses made upon our feelings? Are these admonitions of the Holy Ghost never resisted? Is faith the most natural and obvious thing with these hearts of ours? Let us be reproved and rebuked by this example of the aged saint in the temple. I say, this aged saint. For the days of credulity with him had passed away. Old people are slow to believe new things. They shake their heads at the sanguine hopes and the ready acquiescence of the young in promising enterprises and pretended recent discoveries. The frosts of many winters had extinguished the natural ardors of this old man, and, for him, the sun and the light, and the moon and the stars, were darkened, and the clouds returned after the rain. He was afraid of that which is high, and fears were in his way, and the almond tree flourished, and desire failed, for it was time that he should go to his long home, and for the mourners to go about the streets.

We must agree, then, that, in his circumstances, his faith was a great triumph over unfavorable appearances; indeed, there could not possibly be less to encourage faith than at the moment when he took that child to his arms. Had he the heart of Naaman the Syrian, who went away in a rage from the prophet's door, because he was told to go and wash in Jordan, instead of receiving a cure from the prophet with ceremonious application of his hand to the leprosy, Simeon might have turned away offended, saying, Is this root out of dry ground, my Saviour? Where did he find in that humble scene any thing to gratify his fancy, any thing answering to those pictures with which imagination, perhaps, had filled his mind, while expecting the Lord's Christ? And have I waited for this? is this what Abraham desired to see? is this David's Lord and David's son? is this the burden of Isaiah? There is no beauty in him that I should desire him. It must have been the purest and the strongest faith that made that aged saint feel and act as he did. Love mingled with it, and made his faith perfect; and so, faith, working by love, purified his heart from all those worldly, pompous, and merely Jewish feelings which would have made him despise the infant Messiah. Perhaps he subjected himself to the wonder, if not to the scoffs, of bystanders, taking a young child out of the arms of his mother, a stranger to him, and uttering such words of worship, such unintelligible words — "Mine eyes have seen thy salvation;" "A light to lighten the Gentiles, and the glory of thy people Israel." Blessed saint, we need, and would emulate, thy faith and love. To the world around us Christ yet has no form nor comeliness, and when they see him there is no beauty in him that they should desire him. He is despised and rejected of men. He requires a cross daily of each of his followers. He bids them lay aside resentments, and lusts, and covetousness, which is idolatry, and all worldliness, and to be heavenly minded, and to learn of him who is meek and lowly in heart, that they may find rest unto their souls. Our hearts are slow to take all this to our arms and to our bosoms. We need Simeon's faith and Simeon's love to make us embrace Jesus Christ, with his soul-humbling doctrines and precepts, as he is offered to us in the gospel, and, regardless of the frowns and favors of men, say, Mine eyes have seen thy salvation. We need to be absorbed more in promoting the cause of that Saviour whom Simeon declared to be "a light to lighten the Gentiles, and the glory of the people of Israel." What zeal that good man would have had for the conversion of the world, had he lived in our day. He would have had no rest till every fellow-creature had, by faith and love, seen and embraced the Lord's Christ.

We will make use of Simeon's words to the mother of our Lord for further instruction. We may derive this admonition from the scene before us in the temple:

II. If we dedicate our children to God, we must be prepared to have them suffer great things for the salvation of men.

All Christian parents dedicate their children to God. The forms in which they do it vary, but the consecration of children to the service of God is one of the most natural, as it is a solemn and affecting, duty, and is felt to be a great privilege by pious parents, whether it be attended with a public offering of the children in a religious assembly, or not. When we consecrate our children to God, we must reckon upon great sacrifices and trials, if God will, in their history.

The angel Gabriel appeared to Mary, and said, "Hail, thou that art highly favored among women; the Lord is with thee." Mary afterward exclaimed, in the joy and fulness of her heart, "Henceforth all generations shall call me blessed." Her child grew in stature, and in favor with God and man, and, at length, entered upon his public ministry. Her thoughts and feelings, as a mother, as she heard of his mighty works, his opening the eyes and the ears, and loosing the tongue, and feeding the multitudes, and walking on the sea, and raising the dead, and casting out devils, and healing the sick, can better be imagined than described. These feelings, however, were mixed with other feelings, as she perceived how the chief priests and rulers of the people conspired against him to take his life.

Can we suppose that there never were any of those interviews between them, which a good son, though grown to manhood, loves to have with the mother that bare him? Did he never retreat from the world to her humble dwelling, and tell her of his joys and sorrows; the mighty work which God had given him to do; the toil and pain which marked his daily life; the thronging multitudes and the insidious Pharisee; the love and joy of the Magdalene, and Bartimeus, and the envy and subtle craftiness of the sanhedrim? How did she feel, as she looked upon the marks which care and toil had made upon that child of hers, the object of such wonder in her secret meditations, — for such marks his life of sorrow had made, — "his visage was so marred more than any man's, and his form more than the sons of men." What did that mother want, when she stood without, with his brethren, desiring to speak with him? She saw that things were coming to a crisis with him; her heart was burdened, on his behalf, with a heavy load; all the mother's solicitude, and conscious right to interfere, made her eager to withdraw him from destruction; but her grief swelled like a mountain torrent when she heard that he was betrayed; and where was she, and what were her thoughts and feelings, when the scenes of his mock trial passed on, and he was finally condemned to be crucified? and what sword was that which passed through her own soul also, as she, with the omnipotent energy of a mother's love, stood by and saw him take his place between two thieves, to expire on the accursed tree, as a public malefactor? For we read in John, "Now there stood by the cross of Jesus his mother,"— Enough — no matter who else were there — his mother! O God, our heavenly Father, to what baptisms of sufferings we are called in this world, and how wonderful is that grace which sustains poor creatures like us, under loads which would crush angels, without thine everlasting arm. His mother saw him die — his widowed mother, as we must conclude she was, for the beloved disciple took her, thenceforth, to his own home. "Hail, thou that art highly favored among women," some one at the cross, instigated by the power of darkness, may have whispered, mocking, through her, as she stood by her expiring son, the pretensions of Jesus, and, with him, the fabulous story of his pretended miraculous birth, in the circulation of which she, of course, was implicated. How is it now with thee, O woman? from henceforth shall all generations call thee blessed? O, sad reward of faith and hope! We will not wonder to hear thee echo thy Son's dying cry, My God, my God, why hast thou forsaken me? But, it was for this, though she knew it not, that, in his infancy, she dedicated him to God.

Could you foresee that God would make that little child of yours an instrument of great good, by means of suffering and a dreadful death, would you shrink to consecrate it, by prayer and vows, to God? Dear Christian parents, what an honor it is to have children whom God shall count worthy to suffer for his name's sake. Indifferent servants of God are not selected for this high honor; they are not "counted worthy to suffer;" but God seeks those who, by nature and grace, (both his gift,) are capable of great endurance, superior to the frowns and flatteries of the world, willing to be cast out and trodden under foot by feet that have also trodden under foot the Son of God, ready to suffer the loss of all things, able to bear martyrdom, and to endure unto the end. When we consecrate our children to God, let us fancy that we hear him say to us, Are ye able that the child shall drink of the cup that I drank of, and be baptized with the baptism wherewith I was baptized? Let us say, By thy grace, Lord, we are able. We ask not for them length of days, nor riches, nor favor, nor pleasure, nor to sit on thy right hand and on thy left in thy kingdom, but, that thou wilt qualify them, and employ them, to serve thee, wherever, and in whatever way thou shalt appoint. Then, should we hear even that they are devoured by cannibals whom they go to save, we shall say, Had I now a hundred children, I would give them all to Christ, if he would employ them. The reward is great in heaven; and not only so, but in this world, also, a "hundred fold."

It was so with the mother of Jesus. Weeping endured for a night, but joy came in the morning.

What were her feelings when they told her, Thy son liveth! when she looked into the deserted sepulchre; when Jesus met her; when she stood with him in Olivet, 'all power given unto' him 'in heaven and on earth,' and saw him ascend to his throne in heaven. "Hail, thou that art highly favored among women; all generations shall call thee blessed." If she wished for consolation, and were capable of pride, what must her feelings be at the worship paid her by the millions of the Papal and Greek churches, by kings and nobles, and by the imaginative young devotees of nunneries, who make her their patron saint; — "our lady," "ora pro nobis," "miserere," and all that incense of worship — what reward has she in this, if that could be reward, for all she suffered? Without question, however, it is a sword that is fitted to pierce her more than the nails and spear of her Son's cross, to hear herself worshipped; every "ora pro nobis," every bended knee, every votive offering made to her, is an affliction beyond endurance, were it not that, in heaven, God wipes away all tears from her eyes.

Let us consecrate our children to God, and pray that that holy child Jesus will own them as his servants; then, if they have a fellowship with him in suffering, or serve him amid the temptations and trials of prosperity and ease, to them to live will be Christ; and, when we meet them in heaven, there will be an "over-payment of delight" in saying of them, beloved and honored of Christ, Here am I, and the children which thou hast given me.

III. The words of Simeon, with regard to Christ, teach us that Christ is the great test of human character.

"Behold, this child is set for the fall and rising again of many in Israel — that the thoughts of many hearts may be revealed."

So it came to pass in his day. Some, by means of him, fell, as it were, over a stumbling stone, into perdition. The chief priests and scribes; the amiable young ruler; the man that wished to go and bid them farewell that were at home at his house; those who, on a certain occasion, went away, and walked no more with him, — these were tried as to their secret thoughts and characters, and were found wanting. While, on the other hand, Simeon, and John the

Baptist, and the Eleven, and thousands of the poor and humble, found him to be the Saviour that they needed, for he was meek and lowly in heart, and they were poor in spirit, and theirs was the kingdom of heaven. So they built their hopes upon him for eternity.

Christ is a touchstone to every one of us. What think ye of Christ? is a question whose answer decides the truth or error of our belief. If he be to you only a creature, however exalted, superangelic, but still a creature, your views of the character of God, and of your own character, and of the way to be saved, and of future retribution, must be wrong. If Christ is God, and you worship him, and he made atonement for your sins, this affects the whole character of your belief. "He that hath the Son hath life;" "Whosoever denieth the Son, the same hath not the Father." So with regard to our secret thoughts and our character; tell us how you feel toward Christ, and we will tell you whether you are a Christian, and, if a Christian, what sort of Christian; for this depends on our feelings toward him whose character and whose relation to us, as a Saviour, were intended to affect the human heart more intensely than any thing else. And such is the case. There are no feelings so intense as the feelings which Christ awakens, for or against himself. There was Julian the Apostate, who, falling in battle, seized a handful of sand and flung it toward the sky, saying, Thou hast conquered, O Galilean. Dying Stephen, heedless of the shower of stones, cries, Lord Jesus, receive my spirit. Some are never greatly excited to anger, except by religion; Christ brings no peace to their homes, but a sword. In contrast with them, there are those to whom the name of Christ is music, and they are most happy when they are counted worthy to do any thing for him, and for those who love him. Each of us may see just what we are, by our feelings toward Christ: if we are indifferent, we are opposed to him; we dislike his spiritual character and precepts, and the way to be saved through him. If we love him, we are loved of his Father also. As a proof of all this, we have only to consider that last, dread sentence which Christ says he will pronounce, with the reasons on which it is based: Inasmuch as ye did it, or did it not, to one of the least of these my brethren, ye did it, or did it not, to me. And what follows? "And these shall go away into everlasting punishment, but the righteous into life eternal." Are my feelings toward Christ, indicated by my treatment of those who love him, to settle the question, where I shall spend eternity? Let me see to it, that I think of Christ, and feel toward him, as the word of God requires.

The words of Simeon, as he took the infant

Saviour in his arms, suggest one more remark, which is properly deduced from his feelings and expressions.

IV. We are reminded, by Simeon's experience, that a sight of Christ makes death easy.

There is, most commonly, an effort, with the dying, to be assured of the favor of Christ; and that willingness to die, which so often changes the views and feelings of those who are approaching the grave, is owing, in most cases, to an increased sense of the Saviour's presence. For such purposes, among others, he became flesh, that we, in the hour of weakness and death, might apprehend him, as we cannot apprehend the infinite God. The presence of Christ makes death easy. He comes, and finishes his redeeming work with the believer, at death, and the sight of him makes the Christian willing to depart; and not only willing, but frequently, he says, to depart and be with Christ is far better. Simeon, with Christ in his embrace, longing to die, is a good emblem of a believer on his dying bed, when Christ, whose friend he has been, reveals himself as his Friend.

We, who preach to you, would love, as dying men, to take each of you by the hand, and say, Dear friend, you and we must have a dying bed. We know not how soon we shall find ourselves upon it.

There, the friendship and the presence of Christ is every thing; no matter what your pains are, or whom you are called to part with, the presence of Christ will make death easy. Are you a friend of Christ? When you come to die, may you claim him as a friend, by reason of your friendship to him? To have him show himself to us while the shadows fall between us and time, and to have him whisper, Fear not, for I am with thee, is worth more than a life of sinful pleasure. Be a friend of Christ in your youth, in your prime, in your advanced years, in your declining age. Many a time he will make you feel that he is your Friend, and that promise shall be yours: "AND I WILL NOT BLOT OUT HIS NAME OUT OF THE BOOK OF LIFE, BUT I WILL CONFESS HIS NAME BEFORE MY FATHER, AND BEFORE HIS ANGELS."

SERMON III.

JOHN THE BAPTIST.

MATTHEW XI. 11.

VERILY I SAY UNTO YOU, AMONG THEM THAT ARE BORN OF WOMEN, THERE HATH NOT RISEN A GREATER THAN JOHN THE BAPTIST; NOTWITHSTANDING, HE THAT IS LEAST IN THE KINGDOM OF HEAVEN IS GREATER THAN HE.

WHAT a testimony was this for a man to receive from the Saviour of the world! He is the Judge of character, himself the perfect Man. They who love and serve him have this assurance, that he appreciates and loves every thing in them which is praiseworthy. There is no such honor and happiness as to have the approbation and commendation of Jesus Christ.

As we read this testimony of Christ respecting John, we naturally think of Abraham, and Moses, and Samuel, and David, and Solomon, and Elijah, and Isaiah, seven men who, in their respective classes of character and talent, have no equals in history. But of them, and of all others up to that time, the Saviour says there had not risen a greater than

John the Baptist. Not merely was he the greatest of Prophets, as he certainly was, in being so long predicted and expected; in being the herald of Christ; and in his remarkable knowledge of the Saviour, as expressed in his testimony concerning him; but Christ prefers him to an equality with all who ever lived. He might not, perhaps, write such lyrics as David, or utter such strains of finished eloquence as Isaiah, or possess the quick sagacity of Solomon; but, taking him altogether, the Saviour says he had never had his superior among men. For, though another evangelist represents Christ as speaking of John as the greatest prophet, we must believe that there were intrinsic elements in his character which made him so, in addition to the outward circumstances of his mission. As a man, not merely as a prophet, no one had been greater than he.

With such brief notices of him as we find in the New Testament, we cannot fully analyze his character and determine in what respects, or for what reasons, in particular, he was equal to any mere man. But we know enough to see that he was truly great.

I. John the Baptist was marked by the great strength of his natural faculties, showing itself in energetic, intrepid words and conduct.

It is said of him, "And the child grew, and waxed

strong in spirit, and was in the desert until his showing unto Israel."

It is interesting to notice, in the Scripture biographies, what part solitude had in the formation of character. Abraham goes forth from his home, and dwells in a strange land, a pilgrim and sojourner. Thus his faith grew by living alone with God, and he became the father of all them that believe. Jacob pursues a lonely journey on foot, and sleeps in the field all night; heaven is opened to him, and he vows a vow which, with the vision, decides his whole future life. Moses is a shepherd; he leads his flock to the back side of the desert, and there he comes to Horeb, and sees the burning bush, and, by his solitary meditations and communion with God, is prepared for his eventful work. Elijah was the son of the desert. David had great experience of caves, and dens, and holes in the rock. David's Son and David's Lord must be driven into the wilderness, and be with wild beasts before he can preach. Four, at least, of the first apostles were taken from the solitary and contemplative employment of fishers; and John the Baptist lived in the wilds of Judea, on the locust and the wild honey, covered only with the shaggy cloth of camel's hair, so different from any fabric known to us by that name, his waist girded by no belt from Tyre, or scarf from Persia, but with a leathern thong.

There, in those wilds, from the commencement of

his youth till near the age of thirty, his parents, who were well stricken in years before he was born, being, in all probability, dead, he lived apart from the busy paths of men, not, perhaps, as a hermit, for there were scattered dwellings in that wilderness. He was, however, conversant with the rough face of Nature, in her tangled thickets, dark, pathless woods, overhanging cliffs, swollen streams, diversified, all, with spring-tide beauty, and summer's glory, and autumn's melancholy, and winter's rage; his courage nurtured by darkness and storms, perhaps by conflicts with wild beasts, and by the solemn awe with which solitude and stillness sometimes oppress even the bravest spirit.

Three things, of great importance in his future work, were secured by this solitary life.

He was delivered from the superstitions and corrupting influence of the ecclesiastical rulers, and the sad degeneracy of the times.

He had the best opportunities for religious improvement. He was not idle in that desert; for he, no doubt, spent much time in communion with God — not, perhaps, with frequent enjoyment of visions and dreams, for they, in too great a proportion, would prevent the most vigorous growth of faith; but in fastings, and watchings, and prayers. This prepared him for his work of calling on men to repent. And once more,

His sudden appearance from the desert, with all the marks and influences of an austere life, gave him a power over the popular mind, which he could not have had if he had risen up among those who had been connected with him from childhood. So that he came to the people with all the boldness and authority of a superior being, who had talked with God more than with men.

He came forth, not like the soft, luxurious teachers of his time, nor clothed as they who are in kings' palaces; nor with a supple, pliant spirit — a reed shaken by the wind. The melancholy which hunger brings with it, as in the case of Elijah, he had overcome by an austere mode of life, so that, probably, no man was ever more indifferent and superior to the body than he. His parents could not have failed to tell him of the prophecies which accompanied his birth; his mind must have been filled with premonitions and forecastings of the great work to which he was destined, as the greatest of reformers, and the Spirit of God endued him with a disposition and with feelings which fitted him to be a son of thunder to that corrupt age. Every word of his, even to the last, is marked with decision and energy, to which we scarce find a parallel, while the service he performed required an intrepidity of spirit which is never associated but with the noblest nature.

II. John's true greatness is also seen in his unaffected superiority to the flatteries and frowns of men.

As soon as he began to preach that Messiah's kingdom was at hand, and to call upon the people to receive the rite of baptism, in token of their repentance and preparation to receive Christ, all the people came to him, and among them the scribes and Pharisees. This was a great honor. It was fitted to flatter him, and make him a flatterer. But, with Elijah's spirit before Ahab and Jezebel, he said to them, "O generation of vipers, who hath warned you to flee from the wrath to come?" With no fear of being charged with uncharitableness or illiberality, — one of the severest trials to a tame-spirited, time-serving man, — nor afraid of repulsing his adherents and losing his popularity, nor dreading the imputation of rudeness or rashness, he spake, we may say, as never man spake, to those whose position in society would have made an inferior spirit quail before them. He might truly say with Job, "Did I fear a great multitude, or did the contempt of families terrify me, that I kept silence and went not out at the door?" His boldness and courage were in advance of those qualities in Elijah, who rebuked two crowned heads, and fled from them to the shade of the juniper tree in the desert. John rebuked whole classes of men, and continued to live among them, which was the severest test of moral courage, compelled, as he was, to meet them, day after day, in every mood of his own mind, and of theirs. Instead of feeling complimented at seeing the scholars of his time coming to be baptized of him, and the most esteemed religionists consenting to his ordinance, instead of swerving from his duty, or speaking smooth things, he addressed them, as they deserved, with awful pungency. What a salutation: — "generation of vipers." What a reception to baptism: — "Who hath warned you to flee from the wrath to come?" What an exhortation for Pharisees to hear: — "Bring forth, therefore, fruits meet for repentance." What a threatening: — "And now, therefore, the axe is laid at the root of the tree." Surely, where shall we look for conscious greatness superior to this? The circumstances of his position were such as try and mark the quality of man in a way not surpassed by any thing in human experience.

But after all,

III. The true greatness of John appeared, in a special manner, in his humility.

His mother and the mother of Christ were cousins. But notwithstanding his relationship to Christ, it seems that he did not know him after the period of early youth, even if he did before. He is careful to say more than once, 'And I knew him not; but he that sent me to baptize with water, the same said unto me, This is he.' The reason of this undoubtedly was, to prevent any suspicion of agreement between them as to this popular movement, and to show that it was directed wholly by God. The Spirit had taught him that he was to be the herald, only, of his kinsman; a kinsman younger by half a year than himself, the son of a carpenter, while John was a son of one of the priests; of such an one he must be the herald, and prepare the way for him; for him whose shoe latchet, he, though the greatest of men, would not be worthy to stoop down and unloose.

"Art thou the Christ?" they said to him; "Art thou that prophet?" "No." "Who art thou?" The rulers are ready to acknowledge you in any capacity which you assume. "I am the voice of one crying in the wilderness, Prepare ye the way of the Lord, make his paths straight." Christ appeared. John had gathered personal friends and followers to himself. One day he saw Jesus passing by, and he said to his disciples, "Behold the Lamb of God." He turned their thoughts from himself: "Behold the Lamb of God." Jesus came to him to be baptized. John had never refused to baptize any dignitary of the Jewish church. He would have baptized Annas, or Caiaphas, or whoever was high-priest that year, had he come to him, as perhaps he did; but

Jesus came to him; and John said, "I have need to be baptized of thee, and comest thou to me?" Jesus entered on his ministry. The vast popularity of John had reached its full flood tide. "And they came unto John, and said unto him, Rabbi, he that was with thee beyond Jordan, to whom thou barest witness, behold, the same baptizeth, and all men come to him. John answered and said, A man can receive nothing, except it be given him from God. Ye yourselves bear me witness, that I said, I am not the Christ, but that I am sent before him." He then added these words of tenderness and beauty; — for there is always a degree of softness and delicacy in the sternest nature: "He that hath the bride is the bridegroom; but the friend of the bridegroom, which standeth and heareth him, rejoiceth greatly because of the bridegroom's voice: this my joy, therefore, is fulfilled. He must increase, but I must decrease."

If he that humbleth himself shall be exalted, we very plainly see that there is, at least, probable ground for the declaration of the Saviour respecting John. But the great man passed away. The morning star grew pale, for the sun was up. The friend of the bridegroom is forgotten, for all eyes are directed to the bridegroom himself. He passes away, and finally goes to prison to end his days. His great Lord and Master had begun his wonderful works, and the fame thereof reaches the prison-house of this forerunner. What man of us would not have been tempted to send and know, if, after our self-denying and self-sacrificing efforts in heralding Christ, and preparing the way for him, it was a suitable return that we should be left to languish in Herod's prison? O faith and patience! what a trial! Has Christ, in his zeal for God, forgotten him; in his reception by the people, does he not remember his faithful forerunner? Joseph, in Pharaoh's prison, took care to speak a word for himself to the chief butler, that he should remember Joseph when Pharaoh should lift up his head; but he was forgotten. Has Christ, also, forgotten John? Will not the great and good man send a message to Christ, reminding him that his forerunner is in prison?

He sends a message to him by two of his disciples; but what a message. "Art thou he that should come, or look we for another?" All his thoughts are upon Christ. There is doubt in the minds of critics as to the cause of this question. We are told, that John heard in prison the works of Christ, and sent two of his disciples to him with this inquiry. Some say that this looks like hesitancy on his part with regard to Christ, and that some things in Christ's appearance, without form and comeliness, so different from the common expectation, or, the Saviour's omission to visit him in prison, may have led him to doubt whether Jesus were the Messiah.

But this is incredible. He who had seen the Holy Ghost descending and resting like a dove on Jesus, and who, by a divine impulse, had previously said of him, 'Behold the Lamb of God,' cannot be supposed to have wavered in his confidence that he was the Christ. As to the Saviour's omission to visit his imprisoned friend, we forget that Herod's prison did not enjoy the benignant influences of modern refinement and kindness, and that on no account, probably, would any one, in sympathy with John, have been admitted to his cell. The more probable explanation of John's message to Christ is, that he wished to convince his own disciples that Christ had come, and therefore sent them in an inquiring state of mind, aided by an inquiring message, to see Christ. Not a word of himself, however, have we in this message; his only thought is to detach his followers from himself, and bind them to Christ. Here is true greatness, which has no superior. John is not merely a bold, intrepid reprover and reformer. He is humble and meek, gentle and patient, disinterested and generous, willing to be forgotten and to perish obscurely in the service of his Master. True greatness is always accompanied with childlikeness in the less obvious parts of the character, and appropriate circumstances will always reveal it. John excites our love, as well as our reverence, and He who searches the hearts knew that he was altogether worthy of the greatest commendation.

Christ adds to the declaration, that there is none greater among men than John, this remarkable saying: "Notwithstanding, he that is least in the kingdom of heaven is greater than he."

We cannot understand by this that every humble Christian is superior to John in those things in which John was, by nature and grace, distinguished. But the meaning is this: the humblest Christian who lives under the full influences of the gospel will, by his greater advantages, know more, and be further advanced in those things of which Christ is the revealer, than John, — as a child on a hill can see more than a man in a plain.

John knew nothing, by observation or experience, of the special coming and work of the Holy Spirit. He died before the day of Pentecost, and had no share in the marvels of divine grace and power which accompanied the descent of the Spirit. He was not a witness of the crucifixion and resurrection of his Lord; he knew far less, therefore, than those humble women who, at the sepulchre, learned how life and immortality had been brought to light.

The inferior nature of John's dispensation may be learned from two things. One has already been named; it was antecedent to the descent of the Holy

Ghost, and the beginning of his special work as the third person in the Godhead. And secondly, His baptism was not Christian baptism. That John's baptism was not Christian baptism we learn from the lips of certain of the disciples whom Paul found at Ephesus, and said, Have ye received the Holy Ghost since ye believed? They said, We have not so much as heard whether there be any Holy Ghost. Unto what, then, were ye baptized? They said, Unto John's baptism.

Baptism, in the name of the Father, Son, and Holy Ghost, was not administered till after the ascension of Christ. John's baptism, therefore, was merely a rite by which to impress the minds of the people with the idea of repentance and reformation. The time had not come for men to be initiated into the new dispensation, of which the Father, Son, and Holy Ghost were the proclaimed agents; "for the Holy Ghost was not yet given, because that Jesus was not yet glorified." This baptism, then, being a mere preparatory dispensation, to call attention to Christ and his spiritual kingdom, it is evident that he who enjoys the full privileges of that kingdom is greater than John, even though it be a child, or the humblest servant in the church of Christ, if he but have Christ in him the hope of glory.

The instruction which the character and history of John the Baptist is well suited to impart is this:—

1. *It is the highest honor and privilege to be most intimately identified with the Saviour of the world.*

The greatest of men was appointed to be the immediate herald of Christ. The church of God had, for many centuries, looked for this forerunner to announce the Saviour, and it is deeply interesting and instructive to notice in what terms the annunciation is made. Consider that this man is raised up expressly to make Christ known to men; he, the greatest prophet who had ever appeared, his simple purpose being to tell the world who and what Christ is, and to prepare the way for him. Had the church of God known the moment at which the forerunner would make the annunciation, what intense interest would have been felt, what breathless attention would have been given, while he prepared to utter the first words of his revelation. There was such a moment; and what are the words of annunciation? Let them sink deep into the heart of every human being; let every one, especially, who inquires, concerning Christ, who and what he is, and why he came into the world, attend. John, first looking on Jesus, as he walked, said, "Behold the Lamb of God, which taketh away the sin of the world." These words, spoken in the ears of Jews, had a peculiar significance. A lamb is not a teacher, nor, in the mind of a Jew, an example; a lamb was a sacrifice for sin.

Here, too, was the greatest of those who, up to the moment of his birth, had been born into the world; and we have this testimony from him respecting Jesus: "This is he who, coming after me, is preferred before me, for he was before me." But Jesus was born six months after John: in what way, then, was he before him, except as the preëxistent Word, of whom John evidently speaks when he says again, "He that cometh from heaven is above all. He that is of the earth is earthy, and speaketh of the earth: he that cometh from heaven is above all." Surely we are all prepared with an answer to the question, What think ye of Christ?

The name or title by which a stranger or any distinguished personage is announced to a company, or to the public, is always well considered; the first associations formed with his name being regarded as of importance. The great prophet, sent for no other purpose than to announce the Messiah, and prepare for his reception, inspired, of course, to proclaim, in suitable terms, the character and office of the Saviour, utters, in this one word, the concentrated language of the prophets and the ritual types and ceremonies of four thousand years — LAMB of God: "Behold the Lamb of God, which taketh away the sin of the world."

No honor or privilege had ever been conferred on a man compared with this. Abraham, we may suppose, would gladly have changed places with John; so would Moses, and Elijah, and David. Identified with the Saviour of the world, he is a part of the new dispensation of grace, to the same degree, and for the same reason, that the morning star is a part of the new day. No words of prophets, nor of the sweet Psalmist of Israel, are to be compared with these: 'Behold the Lamb of God;'—behold him, not far off, not through distant years, not in types and shadows: there he is, just by yonder sycamore; he turns the corner of the street; go, speak with him; the Lamb of God is come to take away the sin of the world.

Two of John's disciples heard him speak, and they followed Jesus. Jesus turned, and saw them following, and said unto them, What seek ye? They said unto him, Rabbi, which is, being interpreted, Master, where dwellest thou? He said unto them, Come and see. They came and saw where he dwelt, and abode with him that day, for it was about the tenth hour—a short remnant of a day, from four in the afternoon; but great consequences ensued upon that interview. One of the two which followed Jesus was Andrew, Simon Peter's brother. He first findeth his own brother, Simon, and saith unto him, We have found him of whom Moses, in the law, and the prophets did write. And he brought him to Jesus. John's work is virtually done; he has struck a spark in the hearts of two or three men, which will enlighten the whole world. How interesting and instructive this humble, simple way in which the old dispensation was connected with the new, and then was superseded by it, just by attaching one or two humble, plain men to Jesus Christ.

Who of us may not be a forerunner to Christ, preparing the way for him in some heart, by saying, in the language of instruction, and exhortation, and kind persuasion, Behold the Lamb of God? To the self-righteous, who feel no need of a Mediator, and to whom God appears only as a Father, with no broken law and avenging justice, let us say, in every suitable form, Behold the Lamb of God. To the careless, let us speak of him who came from heaven to put away sin by the sacrifice of himself, and who will come again to judge the world; and to him who labors and is heavy laden let us only say, Behold the Lamb of God. To be identified with Christ and salvation in the mind of one immortal spirit, and, more especially, to be known to Christ as his herald and forerunner, opening the way for him to those for whom he died, is enough to satisfy the ambition of a Cæsar, or Alexander, if directed aright. It is a great honor and privilege to be a minister of Jesus, a missionary, a tract distributer, Sabbath school teacher, visitor of the unevangelized in the town and city, a helper in any and every form of presenting Christ to the minds of men. It should be the business toward which our thoughts and efforts should concentrate, to prepare the way for Christ. All our instructions are vain, unless they lead, in some way, to Christ. Surely it was no great thing for one who felt properly, to say of Christ, in comparison with himself, He must increase, but I must decrease. John did not say this in a sad, murmuring tone, as we should say it of a rival, but with joy at the thought of coming so near to Christ that his light should eclipse him. He was glad to have his own hour of rising so near sunrise. O that we might all of us suffer such eclipse! There is no one who may not, and who should not, in his proper place and sphere, say to others, with every hope of success, Behold the Lamb of God. If permanent reputation, and everlasting remembrance, be sought by us, the surest way to effect it is, to be identified with Jesus Christ. He himself appeals to such a motive, and approves it, when he says, "If any man serve me, let him follow me, and where I am there shall also my servant be; if any man serve me, him shall my Father honor."

2. *The death of this friend of Christ is one of the most affecting and instructive illustrations of God's providence.*

Any one who disbelieved in God, or who could

have supposed John to be an impostor, could not have imagined a death which, in all its circumstances, seemed more directly to contradict the doctrine of the overruling providence of God, or to confute the claims of John, as his messenger. A girl danced before a wicked king, and, in the excitement of the moment, he promised to give her any thing she should ask. Her mother had retained her spite against John, for trying to prevent her own marriage with her brother-in-law, Herod; and though she had obtained his imprisonment, her vengeance was not satisfied. She had instructed the girl what to ask if Herod should be captivated by her; and, straightway, upon Herod's promise and oath, she says, "Give me here the head of John the Baptist in a charger;" and soon the head comes in; the girl takes it, and brings it to her mother.

No doubt she was a most accomplished person, danced well, and moved in the best society, so called; for she lived at court. But the noise of the viol and the tabret has long ago ceased with her, and perhaps, a frantic spirit in hell, she spends eternity with that charger before her eyes always, and that head, the price of her dance, haunting her from one deep to another deep in the bottomless pit. O mother, mother, she cries, you taught me every worldly accomplishment, and also, by your example, to forget God; and brought innocent blood on my soul.

Take this head from before my eyes. Her wretched mother has anguish enough of her own to bear, without the addition of her daughter's curses. Yet will not those curses follow her, and every mother who brings up her daughter for this world only? Are they the only mother and accomplished daughter that will have this present world for their only portion, and endless sorrow at the end of it? "I tell you nay, but, except ye repent, ye shall all likewise perish."

What mischief one wicked girl can do! "She hath cast down many wounded, and many strong men have been slain by her." "Whoso pleaseth God shall escape from her; but the sinner shall be taken by her." "He shall die without instruction, and in the greatness of his folly he shall go astray." If any young friend is dallying with temptation from such a source, "deliver thyself as a bird from the snare of the fowler, and as a roe from the hand of the hunter." "For the ways of man are before the eyes of the Lord, and he pondereth all his goings."

This blessed friend and servant of God was prepared to die; and it was well that he was, for but a very few minutes, probably, intervened between the entrance of the executioner to his cell and the appearance of the ransomed spirit before God. He needed no protracted space between the warning and the stroke of the sword. He was as ready to die instantly as after long notice; and yet, to the eye of man, how sad, how strange. You might say, Will God make no distinction between the righteous and the wicked? No, not in this world, in his providence. "This is one thing," Job says, "therefore I said it: he destroyeth the perfect and the wicked. If the scourge slay suddenly, he will laugh at the trial of the innocent." There is one event to the righteous and to the wicked. John the Baptist, therefore, must not plead exemption from a death which is the mere wanton suggestion of a wanton woman; he must be ready, like all good men, to illustrate, by his own sufferings and death, the great truth, that this life is not a state of reward, but of trial. He must be willing to die in his prime; for he was not over thirty-five years of age, though he is sometimes thought of as a venerable old man, and full of days. He must not refuse to be carried to the grave a headless trunk. Whether Herodias shall pierce his tongue with her bodkin, or whether his head shall be devoured by dogs, or be thrown into the Jordan, John must yield himself to that law of providence which does not discriminate between the evil and the good.

Jonathan Edwards, than whom, of all that are born of women, there is none greater in intellectual endowments, must submit, to have that earthly tabernacle of his destroyed by the loathsome and hideous small-pox, as well as the most common and ordinary of his fellow-men. And yet we read, and still it is true, "Precious, in the sight of the Lord, is the death of his saints." God did not cast off these servants of his; and the outward circumstances of their death were really not worth regarding, by them nor by Him, compared with the far more exceeding and eternal weight of glory which awaited them. We are taught by this that, to him who is a true friend of Christ, death is easy with the head on a block, or the body wrapped in flames, or covered with honey to attract the bees and wasps, or smothered in a bag with snakes, or sawn asunder with a saw of wood; while, to one who has no Saviour whom he has befriended, it is hard to die on the softest and richest bed of down, unless this greatest curse be added to that dying bed of the sinner, that "there are no bands in his death," but with peace and with apparent resignation, like that smooth brim of the cataract just where it bends over to the abyss, he falls asleep, and wakes in hell.

3. *The prominent doctrines and exhortations of such a man as we have seen John to be, deserve our most serious consideration.*

We have already considered the testimony which he gave to the preëxistence of Christ, and to the great object of his coming, namely, to make atonement for sin. We may also notice his designation of Christ as a purifier of his church.

He represents him as having a husbandman's fan, with which he would thoroughly purge his threshing floor, gather the wheat into his garner, and burn up the chaff with unquenchable fire. Now, Christ is the same yesterday, to-day, and forever. He has not come to save men in their sins, but from their sins. We may not plead that we have pious parents, or pious relatives in our ancestral line; for God can of the stones raise up heirs of grace. Nor can we plead, I am a member of the church; for 'now, also, the axe is laid at the root of the tree; every tree, therefore, which bringeth not forth good fruit, is hewn down, and cast into the fire.'

We are also instructed by this great and faithful servant of Christ, and by what Christ says of our privileges, — making us greater, in some respects, than John, if we improve them, — that it is a solemn thing to live under such privileges as we enjoy in these days. What accumulated testimony, from heathen lands, to the truth and power of the gospel; what instructions are we furnished with by the religious press; what calls, in revivals of religion — the Spirit and the bride saying, Come. John closes up his testimony, with regard to Christ, with these words: "The Father loveth the Son, and hath given all things into his hands. He that believeth on the Son hath everlasting life, and he that believeth not the Son shall not see life, but the wrath of God abideth on him." Do I believe, or does the wrath of God abide upon me?

Would we testify our love for this friend of Christ, we can do nothing more appropriate than to obey him, as, by his words left on record, he seeks to lead us to Christ. Let us say, as his hearers did, "And what shall we do?" How faithfully he would speak, and tell us to bring forth works meet for repentance; to break off sin by righteousness, and iniquity by turning unto God. How he would terrify sinners, by exposing their secret wickedness, and ringing the alarms of death and hell in their ears. How he would urge the awakened to go, without delay, to Christ, the Lamb of God. And how he would weep over some who have long refused Christ, saying of him, "And no man receiveth his testimony."

Herod, hearing of Christ, said, "John have I beheaded, but who is this of whom I hear such things? And he desired to see him." You shall see him, Herod, when he comes in the clouds, and brings with him those that sleep in Jesus. You shall see, also, the man whom you beheaded, 'risen from the dead,' as your guilty conscience once made you fear was the case before. And there, at that dread tribunal, where John and Herod are to meet once more, each of us must appear, and each of us be assigned to the company of Herod, or of John, for eternity; — to which of them, will be decided by the question, Am I a friend of Christ? How this question would be answered, if we were pressed to a decision now, may be seen by this consideration: If called suddenly to a dying man who should ask, "What must I do to be saved?" could I, from my own experience, say, Behold the Lamb of God? If not, the forerunner has spoken to us, the Lamb of God has been offered for us, thus far, in vain. If we cannot point a dying sinner to Christ, what shall we do when we are dying? How can we hope to cast our anchor then 'within the veil, WHITHER THE' GREAT 'FORERUNNER HATH FOR US ENTERED'?

SERMON IV.

THE BRIDEGROOM AND BRIDE AT CANA.

JOHN II. 1, 2.

AND THE THIRD DAY THERE WAS A MARRIAGE IN CANA OF GALILEE; AND THE MOTHER OF JESUS WAS THERE. AND BOTH JESUS WAS CALLED, AND HIS DISCIPLES, TO THE MARRIAGE.

In a humble town of Palestine, more than eighteen hundred years ago, a marriage took place which has been more widely known, and more permanently remembered, than the nuptials of any other human pair. More eyes have read the account of it, more ears have listened to the story of its interesting incidents, than all the royal weddings of the world can boast; and hearts which were never filled with emotion by hearing of oriental nuptials, have been interested by the account of this wedding. It will continue to be read and pondered when the impressions of every brilliant, imposing pageantry have passed away; nor will any future marriage occupy such a place in history.

The cause of the celebrity given to this wedding

at Cana was simply this—that the Saviour was invited to be present. It is the only marriage ever mentioned to which the parties called him. "And both Jesus was called, and his disciples, to the marriage." The mother of Jesus seems to have been there as a matter of course. It was not a matter of course that her Son should be invited; but, for some reason, an invitation was extended to him, and not only so, but (as we may suppose, from regard to him) three strangers from other places, Andrew, Peter, and Philip, who had attached themselves to him as his personal friends and disciples, were invited to attend. It is no unwarrantable presumption that this bridegroom and bride were friends of Christ; we may, accordingly, reckon them with those whose characters or actions we are considering in these discourses.

The account of this wedding is given for the purpose of relating the beginning of the Saviour's miracles. For some reason, the wine was deficient. We are not informed whether this was owing to the failure of a tradesman to keep an engagement, or to a mistake on the part of the provider, or to an unexpected increase in the number of guests. The mother of Jesus told him of the casualty, with the view of obtaining a supply by his miraculous power. His answer had nothing disrespectful in it. The appellation, 'Woman,' was the common oriental form of address, even to persons of high degree; and the Saviour uses it when, on the cross, he turned the attention of his mother to John, saying, "Woman, behold thy Son." The expression, "What have I to do with thee?" does not have, in the original, precisely the tone which the English words seem to express; but the translation is as near as any English phrase could approach to the exceedingly condensed form of expression. It was a mode of signifying an unwillingness to be interfered with, or dictated to, joined with some disapprobation. But in the case before us, the intimation annexed, that Christ would work a miracle, the time of which had not yet come, softens the disapprobation. There was evidently good reason for such disapprobation on the part of Christ. His mother sought to make an irreverent use of his divine power. She did not seek for a miracle that God might be honored, nor that the spectators might receive spiritual benefit; but she applied to her Son in some such way as she would have applied to a magician. All that she thought of was the consternation of her friends at finding that the principal means of entertaining the company had failed, and, therefore, she requested her Son to exert his miraculous power, and help them out of their difficulty. That this was her purpose in what she said to Christ, and not merely to make the casual remark, that the wine had failed, we learn from her secret admonition to the servants, "Whatsoever he saith unto you, do it," showing that she still expected him to work a miracle.

It was derogatory to the Saviour's character and office, that he should be a repairer of accidents, and put forth divine power merely to gratify wishes which had no higher end than relief from awkward embarrassments. Such was the limit of his mother's motives, and the Saviour stands before us in the true dignity of his nature and office, in reproving such motives. Whatever he may see fit to do afterward, let no one think that he is a mere convenient servant. He went to that wedding to work a miracle. He reproved the improper feelings and motives of his mother, and yet informed her that he should, in time, accomplish his purpose. Strange, that, after reading and considering this, so large a portion of our race have insisted on using Mary's advocacy with her Son in heaven, saying, Mother, command thy Son; and this addressed to one who showed herself to be an erring mortal, deserving of the Saviour's calm, respectful, dignified reproof.

Jesus proceeded to do as he had purposed, and changed a large quantity of water into wine. Six water pots of stone, used instead of cisterns or reservoirs, holding each about nine gallons of our measure, and kept near at hand, on account of the superstitious or ceremonial habits of the people to wash often, (as the evangelist says, "after the manner of the purifying of the Jews,") stood within or near the house. The servants were commanded by the Saviour to fill them with water; and they filled them (by his direction, no doubt) to the brim, leaving no ground for suspicion of any admixture. Without pronouncing any words of charm or incantation, Christ simply told the servants to draw, and to present the draught to him who presided at the table, usually some friend of the parties. He had, officially, a deep interest in the proceedings, and, on this occasion, unwittingly gave the strongest testimony to the perfection of the miracle.

The evangelist adds the following words to this account: "This beginning of miracles did Jesus in Cana of Galilee, and manifested forth his glory, and his disciples believed on him."

There is useful instruction to be derived from the simple act of this bridegroom and bride at Cana, in calling Christ to their wedding, and from his presence there.

I. As Christ began his miracles at a wedding, we may infer that he, and his religion, are friendly to human happiness.

It cannot be supposed that it was by mere accident that the Saviour began his miracles at a wedding, rather than at the grave of Lazarus, or the gates of Nain. His brief sojourn on earth, after he had entered on his ministry, was only three years and a half. Now, considering what an eventful life that was to be, constituting the New Testament history, forming the basis for the opinions and feelings of all coming generations with regard to him, it was, no doubt, viewed, by infinite wisdom, as of the first importance that all his public acts should be arranged with regard to the best effect upon the great end for which he came into the world. Thus, though his daily life seems wholly unpremeditated, his great works accidental, depending only on his happening to meet this or that object of compassion, we must suppose that all was planned beforehand, and that it was the suggestion of divine wisdom and goodness that he should begin his miracles at a scene which, more than any other, interests every one, of whatever time or nation. The Saviour takes his place by the side of a bridegroom and bride, and at their wedding, in their presence, and for their happiness, he first manifests forth his glory; and his disciples, who had thus far believed through the testimony of John the Baptist, now receive him and testify of him as the Christ, from their own knowledge. He could have produced this effect on them and others, by casting out a devil, or destroying a herd of swine, or by curing the palsy, or opening a grave. "How great is his wisdom, and how great is his beauty." He goes to a wedding; he meets the human race, whom he came to bless, first of all, at a nuptial ceremony. He mingles his sympathies with their joys, before he mourns with them in their sorrows. He thus tells them that he has not come to look on the dark side of their condition alone, but to take a just view of it; to rejoice with them that rejoice, as well as to weep with them that weep, recognizing the truth, that there is much in this world to make us happy, and nothing more so than the love of kindred hearts, united in those bonds which the benevolent Creator constituted in Paradise. He has come to deliver us from hell, and he wishes us to know that there is a heaven. We are subject to miseries innumerable and great, our danger is fearful, our liability to eternal sorrow is alarming; but other things also are true, — that God loves us with a benevolent and compassionate love, seeks our perfect happiness, and would restore us to that which our first parents lost by the fall; and not only would he make us happy hereafter; he wishes us to know that the ways of wisdom, here, are ways of pleasantness, and all her paths are peace; that religion is not only consistent with present happiness, but eminently promotes it; that Christ and religion do not frown upon human joys, but, on the contrary, purify them, hallow them, impart a zest to them, and give with them that richest and sweetest ingredient, a sense of God's approbation and love.

So that if any are tempted to look upon religion as an enemy to innocent pleasure, and feel that to be followers of Christ is to take the veil; that to enter the Christian church is to shake hands at the door with every innocent mirth; that putting on the new man is to put on stiffness and austerity; that being converted is being made unfit for social life; and that religion means the surrendering of every thing and gaining nothing, they may see their error corrected by this testimony of Christ our Saviour, in favor of human happiness, in his being present at a wedding, and in his beginning the work for which he came from heaven by contributing to the hilarity of a wedding feast. So far from being unfriendly to human happiness, religion alone warrants and enables us to be perfectly happy in this world. The church of Christ is spoken of in the Bible as the only portion of the human race that have claims to perfect happiness. Christians are represented, by this same figure of marriage, as raised to the height of earthly happiness, in being the bride of Christ. Is this an austere, melancholy creature, that comes floating by us on the wings of fancy, to whom are addressed such words as these: "All thy garments smell of myrrh, and aloes, and cassia, out of the ivory palaces whereby they have made thee glad;" "The king's daughter is all glorious within; her clothing is of wrought gold"? Though spiritual things, it might be said, are designated by these metaphors, which describe the church of God in its holiness and happiness, yet if such effects, pictured by such images of beauty, can be the result of religious joy, surely religion is eminently favorable to the highest bliss.

But religion, it is said, forbids us to frequent playhouses, and frowns on dancing between the sexes. There is a great mistake here. Religion is not responsible for making these things obnoxious. Must a man or woman be a Christian in order to feel disapprobation of waltzing? Do none but church members think that such a thing is unsuitable? Do we need to be converted before we can disapprove of things which the devotees of Juggernaut's temple, and before his blood-stained car, practise; are Christians only blessed with the light of nature, to disallow things which the light of nature surely condemns? Were we to argue against theatres, we would not, or we need not, quote one passage of the Bible; for wise and good men and women, out of the Christian church, are among the very best authorities as to the pernicious effect of playacting; and with regard to novels, (not, simply, works of imagination,) pernicious, not for the imagination in them, but for exaggerated, false views of things, and for the bad effect, even when they are true, of dwelling too much upon fictitious scenes, if one were to preach against reading novels, so called, and should quote the Bible, he would perhaps, first of all, cite from it a quotation which Paul makes from a heathen poet; for he quotes Euripides, or Menander, for they both have it, when he says, "Evil communications corrupt good manners."

Let not the friends of promiscuous dancing, and of theatres, and of certain novels, lay their condemnation at the door of religion; they are tried and condemned, as it were, in the Common Pleas of moral sentiments, not first of all in the higher judicatory of religion; though if they take their appeal to that, the judgment of the lower court will certainly be affirmed against them.

While with their knowledge of their own hearts, compared with the holiness of God, and with their self-disapprobation, and with opposition, from the world around them, to that which they hold most dear, Christians, if in this life only they had hope in Christ, would of all men be the most miserable, yet, with the hope of future blessedness, which enters greatly into all their present joys, and assures them that their faith is not in vain, Christians are of all men the happiest, and the most to be envied. Take them in the moments of their highest earthly joy, when their best earthly affections are crowned with all that heart can wish. A Christian, from those heights of happiness which, to an unregenerate man, are the highest conceivable, can say, There is a happiness, now, and hereafter, which is superior to this. 'O God, thou art my God.' 'Whom have I in heaven but thee? and there is none upon earth that I desire beside thee.' Sometimes, in the midst of the highest earthly joys, we are visited by this feeling; — 'After all, this does not satisfy me; my soul craves something else.' It may be said of every form of earthly pleasure, "Whoso drinketh of this water shall thirst again." And is there any thing else more satisfying than the highest earthly joy? Yes, and something which leaves no desire unsatisfied. And here we have the explanation of those wonderful words of Christ, which none can properly understand till they experience the truth of them: "I am the bread of life. He that cometh to me shall never hunger, and he that believeth on me shall never thirst." Religion alone satisfies the wants of the soul; it is an addition to every form of human happiness; there is not one human joy which is not made richer and sweeter by the consciousness that, with it, we have peace with God. Then, too, the thoughts of change, and decay, and the end of every fond enjoyment, will come unbidden into every bower of earthly happiness; and the Christian alone can triumph over such thoughts, knowing that the happiness which is above all to him, is superior to time, and change. and death; for "things present and things to come all are yours — and ye are Christ's, and Christ is God's."

We have not followed cunningly-devised fables, and we have no private end to secure, when we say to you that, if you would be truly happy in this world, you must be a Christian. We would select some young friend, whose prospects are the fairest, and whose present happiness is all which the world can ever give, and would say to that young friend, Your happiness is greatly deficient. One thing thou lackest. Thousands like you have 'clasped these phantoms, and have found them air.' Jesus said to the people around him, "Your fathers did eat manna in the wilderness, and are dead." So we may say to you, These joys seem to you like angels' food, but all before us, who have fed upon them, nevertheless are dead. All like you who have had the world for their chief good, 'did eat manna in the wilderness;' and what are they the better for it? they had not that bread from heaven, but Christ giveth you that true bread from heaven.

It is deeply affecting to think of those who had this world for their portion, and lived in pleasure, finding, in another world, that Christians were, even in this life, happier than they; but they received their good things, as they esteemed them, and likewise Christians evil things in their conflicts with evil, but now they are comforted, while the sinner is tormented. What a different thing religion will seem to many in another world. Here they connect it only with austerity, self-denial, weeping; all seems cold and repulsive to them. How will it seem when the beauty of the Lord our God is upon us, when every form and every face is angelic — nay, more than this — like Christ, for "we shall be like him;" — when our dwelling-place is the metropolis of suns and stars, where the God of creation has lavished the exceeding riches of his power and skill; "where angels walk and seraphs are the warders;" where we shall have music, and eloquence, and genius, and landscapes, and travels, and society, and friendships, and great congregations, and homes, and friends restored to each other; and the walls, and foundations, and gates, and pavements of our place of habitation shall be of prodigal affluence, but forgotten by us in the incomparable joys of the heart and mind? Is this the Christian's heaven? the lost sinner, the devotee of fashion, the voluptuous man, will say; have Christians gained all this by their religion? Their happiness, in full tide, is just beginning, for eternity, and ours is ended. Then they will lie down in sorrow; but they were forewarned of this, and were assured that godliness has "the promise of this life and of that which is to come."

And yet the Saviour himself complained that while he tried to make men feel that religion was something cheerful, and fitted to make them perfectly happy, he was repulsed by them, as much as when he warned them of the consequences of sin. "Whereunto," he says "shall I liken this generation?" For the burden of John's mission was repentance and reformation; and he enforced it by his own austere life; but this repulsed them, when the excitement of novelty was over, and they said, 'He hath a devil;' he is so peculiar, such a bigot, frowning upon every worldly pleasure, denouncing us with such vehemence, and living in such a supernatural way, that he must be possessed. The Son of man came eating and drinking, that is, like other people; he began his public ministry at a wedding, and the first thing which he did was to create the means of a festive entertainment. Did he suit the tastes and wishes of men any better? "And they said, Behold a man gluttonous, and a wine bibber, a friend of publicans and sinners. But wisdom is justified of her children." Every one who is truly wise will appreciate the wisdom of his course in trying to conciliate men by being cheerful and kind, though, alas! to no purpose. But let the disposition of Christ, as presented to us in this narrative, convince every one that the nature of religion is cheerful, and intended to make men happy; that the path of the just is like the shining light; and that a happy Christian life, with heaven at the end of it, is better than a life of sin with hell for its reward. If you will begin a religious life, if you will make Christ your friend, and be a friend to him, he will surprise you with the blessings of goodness, and with his power to make you happier, infinitely happier, even in this life, than the world can ever do.

See that bright and cheerful face of the ruler of the feast, at the head of the table, after he has tasted Christ's wine. He beckons to the bridegroom, and compliments him upon his affluent, generous conduct to his guests. Thus many a friend of yours gets praise from you, and gratitude, for goodness and kindness which are Christ's doings. O that you could see his hand and his heart in all that makes your life happy, and be persuaded that he is the best of friends, and that to be a friend of his is the best relation and character which you can sustain.

II. The Saviour should be a specially invited guest at every wedding.

In the first place, he is willing to come and to be wherever his friends are. He is with them in prison, and poverty, and sickness, and in the valley of death, by his special presence; and will he not rejoice with them that do rejoice, as well as weep with them that weep? Yes; for, In the second place, he has testified his great interest in marriage by beginning his public ministry at a wedding. It was not a royal wedding.

It was not even in Jerusalem. The place is not mentioned in the Old Testament; for Kanah was in the tribe of Asher; but this Cana, in Zebulon. It was the Saviour's interest in marriage, as relating to the welfare and happiness of the whole human family, that brought him to that wedding. He is that Creator, whose first miracle, in the beginning of the old world, was the creation of a companion for man; and now, as he brings in the new creation, his first miracle is at a marriage. How can we forget and neglect him in this transaction? If we ever need the Saviour's blessing and love, we need it, and it is specially precious, in that transaction which, more than any other, affects the whole life.

But, perhaps, when this great event of our lives was taking place, some of us forgot the Saviour. We made a careful scrutiny as to the guests whom we ought to invite, or whom we thought that we should gratify with an invitation; and we were extremely careful to give no offence by any neglect or slight, knowing how keenly such a thing at such a time is felt. But, of all our friends, there was one whom, perhaps, after all, we neglected; and he was the very best friend we had. Perhaps he had more to do with the acquaintance and love which led to our marriage than any other; he took pleasure in the progress of events, and brought them to their consummation; and when the happy day came, and every friend, who had a claim, was present, and all was bright and joyous, he was neglected, and was not so much as thought of as one of the guests.

And yet it might truly have been said to those guests, as John the Baptist said of Christ, "There standeth one among you whom ye know not." Christ was there, an unwelcomed, unthought-of spectator. He looked upon the company, the bridegroom, and the bride; and may he not have said to himself, They do not know that I loved them before they loved each other; loved them, and gave myself for them; and that all they enjoy is the fruit of my love and sufferings for them. How much they need my friendship. Once, and but a little while since, they were utter strangers to each other. This union is earthly; it breaks asunder at the touch of death; could they but love me, were they my friends, they would have in me a security to their present bliss, and heaven to crown them at the end.

Months and years have rolled away, and how has it fared with us, in this relation? Some of you had Christ for an invited guest on the occasion of your marriage; and if you have since, consistently with this, acknowledged him in all your ways, he has blessed you, making you happy in your union, smoothing those little asperities which happen to all, and which, sometimes, grow to alienation and bitter sorrow. In times of affliction he has rewarded you, for your love to him, by a peace that passeth all understanding.

If we have not been happy, if domestic trials and sorrows have made our path gloomy, let us only recollect whether we called the Saviour to the wedding. Some contract marriage without thinking of their God and Saviour in connection with it; but, on the contrary, a suggestion that his guidance and his approbation are essential to happiness, is regarded as interfering with their feelings, and marring their pleasure. Religion is most unwelcome, to many, in these seasons of pleasurable acquaintanceship and the interchange of hearts. What a mistake to think that he who is called "Wonderful, Counsellor, the Mighty God," is out of place in giving us counsel about our intentions of marriage. One humble, heartfelt prayer to Christ, in connection with this important step, would, in thousands of cases, have prevented anguish of soul from which there has been no refuge but the grave.

The Saviour, whether called, or not, to the wedding, heard the vows we uttered, as we took and gave the right hand, and, calling God to witness, swore to be faithful to each other till death. Many who were witnesses of your marriage (in some instances, O, how many) have gone the way of all the earth; but Christ was there; Christ is a witness of the vows, and of the manner in which they have been kept. His approbation of our kindness, forbearance, gentleness, faithfulness, and love unfeigned, in this relation, is indispensable to peace and happiness. There is no one who can appreciate such things like Christ.

Christ is one day to have a marriage of his own. The announcement will soon be heard, "Let us rejoice, and be glad, and give honor to him; for the marriage of the Lamb is come, and the bride hath made herself ready." She has been seen by one who has made a report of her, a messenger being sent to him to say, 'Come up hither; I will show thee the bride, the Lamb's wife.' He saw the city which the bridegroom had built for her, compared with which the city that Solomon built for Pharaoh's daughter was a dark place. There never was such a bride as this; and all the weddings of earth, should they combine their festivities and brilliancy, would not be seen nor thought of in that exceeding great joy. Jesus Christ is to be publicly united, before the universe, to this bride, and, through eternity, is to rejoice over her with joy, and rest in his love. Bunyan, when, in his dream, he saw the gates of heaven shut, after the arrival of the pilgrims, says, 'which, when I saw, I wished myself among them.' I feel the same desire. I want to see that marriage. I have been invited, and I am happy to say I have, in my hands, an invitation for each of you, which I now deliver, signed and sealed with the Saviour's own hand. Let no man's heart fail him at the thought of having slighted Christ in the matter of his own marriage, for it is not too late, even now, to repair the injury. If the anniversary of your wedding is near, let that day be a time of special prayer, and reconciliation with this beloved, heavenly Friend. Whether it be near, or at some distance, go this day with her who, with you, neglected Christ on that occasion, and, hand in hand, kneel before him, and implore his presence and his blessing for the remainder of your way. But, if that companion be no more, seek him who knows all your history; and, in the multitude of your thoughts within you, his comforts will delight your soul.

Many a scene of joy and gladness will yet be celebrated by many to whom I have the pleasure to preach. Let me charge you to take no step in such a transaction without making Christ your Friend and Counsellor. He will be specially interested in all that you propose, and in all that is proposed to you, in such connection. Make Christ one of your guests. Send to him by special prayer, and, with your chosen friend and future companion, say to him, 'If thy presence go not with us, carry us not up hence.' We read in the subsequent history of Christ, 'So Jesus came again into Cana, where he made the water wine.' Can we doubt that his interest in that transaction, and in those friends who bade him to their wedding, led him to visit them in their abode? Thus, though your dwelling be like humble Cana, and you, like the bridegroom and bride there, may not be widely known, Jesus, being specially honored by you in the beginning of your marriage relation, will often visit your abode, turn every common pleasure of your life into a witness that his hand is in it, and seal your earthly happiness by enabling you to appropriate those words: "BLESSED ARE THEY WHICH ARE CALLED UNTO THE MARRIAGE SUPPER OF THE LAMB."

SERMON V.

THE TWELVE APOSTLES.

REVELATION XXI. 14.

AND THE WALL OF THE CITY HAD TWELVE FOUNDATIONS, AND IN THEM THE NAMES OF THE TWELVE APOSTLES OF THE LAMB.

THE object of the representation in the text is, no doubt, in part, to bestow exceeding honor upon the apostles of Christ. Heaven is represented as a city, with a wall great and high, with twelve courses of foundation stones, most precious; and conspicuous in those twelve stones are inscribed, here and there, the names of the apostles. It would be difficult to conceive of a greater mark of honor. The builders of cities are celebrated in history, but here are men whose names are associated with the very foundations of that heavenly city, the "new Jerusalem," "which is above all." We will consider

I. THE CALL OF THESE MEN TO THE APOSTLESHIP. The Saviour, after that John was put in prison, came into Galilee, "preaching the gospel of the kingdom of God, and saying, The time is fulfilled, and the kingdom of God is at hand; repent ye, and believe the gospel." Walking by the Sea of Galilee, he saw "Simon Peter and Andrew his brother casting a net into the sea, for they were fishers. And Jesus said unto them, Follow me, and I will make you to become fishers of men. And straightway they forsook their nets, and followed him."

There had been a previous interview between him and these two men, in consequence of the words spoken by John the Baptist to Andrew and another. Simon had been brought by Andrew, his brother, to Christ, and Christ had surnamed him Peter. They had not, however, followed him constantly, as disciples, till they were called from their boat, on the same day that the two sons of Zebedee, James and John, received a similar call from their boat, and followed Christ. These were with their father in the ship, "mending their nets; and they left their father in the ship with the hired servants, and went after him." Their mother was Salome.

Passing by the place where the customs were received, Christ saw Matthew sitting at his business, and he said, "Follow me;" and he arose, left all, and followed him. Matthew is also called Levi, who made a feast for Christ, and many publicans sat down with him. The day following the interview with Andrew and Peter, Jesus "would go forth into

Galilee, and findeth Philip, and saith unto him, Follow me."

These six disciples are all of the twelve of whose call we have any account. The other six are these: —

BARTHOLOMEW, of whom we know nothing. Some, indeed, suppose that he was the same as Nathanael of Cana, because he is mentioned by John, in the last chapter of his Gospel, as present, with the disciples, when Christ appeared to them, and ate with them, on the sea shore. But this is a mere supposition.

SIMON, the Canaanite, or Zelotes, — not that he was from Cana, but the word, Canaanite, is a Syro-Chaldaic word, whose Greek translation is, Zelotes, or a man of zeal. The sect of "Zealots," so called, were men distinguished for their zeal in sustaining Jewish institutions, and procuring the punishment of offences against the ceremonial law and the traditions of the elders; though the sect did not prevail, to any great extent, till just before the destruction of Jerusalem. Of this Simon, also, we know nothing; it being probable that in all the cases in which Simon is named, Peter is intended, as being the elder of the two. It is doubtful whether he is the Simon, as some think he is, who was named by the Jews, on one occasion, with James, and Joses, and Jude, as the brother of our Lord, or (as we know that the name, in this connection, means) his kinsman. — The next two were brothers.

James, the son of Alpheus, (or Cleophas,) was the cousin of Jesus, being the son of 'the other Mary.' He is called James the Less, or the younger, to distinguish him from the brother of John. James the Less was the writer of one of the Epistles.

Lebbeus, or Thaddeus, is Jude, who also wrote one of the Epistles. It was he who asked the question, "Lord, how is it that thou wilt manifest thyself unto us, and not unto the world?"

Thomas, translated Didymus, or a twin, is known to us chiefly by his doubts respecting the resurrection of Christ, and his subsequent exclamation, "My Lord and my God."

Judas Iscariot is so called from his belonging to a place called Kerioth, in the tribe of Judah, — Ish Carioth, (or Is Cariot,) meaning a man of Carioth.

When and how these six were called to be disciples of Christ, we do not learn. Their appointment with the other six, as the twelve apostles, is distinctly mentioned. A disciple is a learner; an apostle is a messenger; and the time came for Christ to select from his disciples, or attendant learners, some whom he should commission as apostles.

Their appointment is thus mentioned by the evangelist Luke: "And it came to pass, in those days, that he went out into a mountain to pray, and continued all night in prayer to God. And when it was day, he called unto him his disciples, and of them he chose twelve, whom he also named apostles."

The selection and appointment of the twelve apostles was preceded by a whole night of prayer. Even the perfect man, Christ Jesus, would not approach so momentous a work as the selection of those who were to be the inspired apostles, without prayer, and that of no ordinary kind. On the morrow, he had purposed to make choice of the men to whom all succeeding generations would look, as the first authorized expounders of the Christian religion. Never was the selection of cabinet ministers and privy councillors, ambassadors, or commissioners, so important as that selection of the apostles, the prime ministers of a kingdom which was to be an everlasting kingdom; ambassadors, on the high concerns of eternity, between God and man. The great importance of this selection, perhaps, kept the Saviour awake all night, and, in communion with God, he sought and obtained direction. Here is an instance in which his human nature is seen to retain all its dependence, its need of prayer and of divine guidance; the presence, in his person, of the divine Word, never confounding the distinction between the human and the divine, but leaving him still 'the man Christ Jesus.' And let us note, that, if such as he needed to pray, and if he spent so much time in prayer to qualify himself for important transactions in his earthly life, we cannot safely perform our duties, and, especially, we cannot discharge important trusts com mitted to us, unless we pray in a manner that shows us to be in earnest, with much deliberation and reflection, and repeated and protracted waiting upon God. There is nothing more profitable for one who has a solemn and important duty to perform, or question to settle, or difficulty to manage, than to retire for a longer time than an ordinary season of devotion, and spend it with God. All who have been eminently blessed as useful men, refer to such seasons as having had an important connection with their success. If churches seeking pastors were to meet frequently for special prayer, and, while using proper means to obtain information respecting candidates, would place their chief dependence on Him who, at his ascension, received such "gifts for men," they would imitate him in his selection of his first ministers.

Having appointed these twelve disciples, the first thing which he did, as we learn from Luke, was, to deliver in their hearing, addressing himself specially to them, the Sermon on the Mount. In this, he unfolded to them some of the first principles of his religion, as they were able to bear them, deferring the more important mysteries, the deep things of God, till after his ascension, when they should have been with him longer, and thus be fully prepared for truths which, with their ignorance and Jewish notions, they would not have been able to receive. Having kept them for about three years with him, taking advantage of every event to instruct them and to correct them, sometimes reproving and even chiding them, but always treating them with affection, the time came for him to leave them; and we may easily imagine the sorrow with which the announcement of that purpose filled their hearts. The account of the farewell scenes between him and them, beginning with the celebration of the last passover, and his discourse to them, and the last prayer on that occasion, are not surpassed in interest and instructiveness by any thing in the Saviour's life. He finally stood with them on Mount Olivet, and gave them their great commission to go 'into all the world and preach the gospel to every creature'; and it came to pass, while he blessed them, that he was parted from them, and carried up into heaven, and a cloud received him out of their sight.

At an early meeting after the ascension of their Lord, they proceeded to fill the vacancy made by the apostasy and death of Judas, and chose Matthias by lot; but no mention is afterward made of him; and this has led some strangely to question whether they did not transcend their duty and the necessities of the case, and whether it was not intended that the place

10

of Judas should continue vacant, or be filled by the apostle Paul. But all this implies a doubt of their inspiration. The New Testament is also silent with regard to the life and labors of Bartholomew, and Simon Zelotes. That the place of Judas was to be filled, we learn from the Psalm quoted by Peter at the election of a new apostle; quoted, surely, not as a verse of poetry, having a mere accidental resemblance to the case, but as an inspired prophecy, saying of Judas, "Let his habitation be desolate, and his bishopric let another take." Paul was appointed independently of any connection with the original apostles, for special reasons, as a new, independent witness for Christ, which he takes pains to insist upon, where he says, that, when it pleased God who had separated him from his birth, "to reveal his Son in me, immediately I conferred not with flesh and blood, neither went I up to Jerusalem, to them that were apostles before me." We cannot reasonably question that Matthias was divinely designated to complete the number of the twelve, after that Judas had gone to his own place. Fame or notoriety is not essential to usefulness or acceptableness with God. The labors and faith of those apostles who have no reward in the applause of men, were not disregarded or forgotten by Him unto whom 'belongeth mercy; for he rendereth to every man according to his work.'

II. The first apostles are an illustration of that sovereign love in Christ which is independent of human merit.

"Ye have not chosen me, but I have chosen you, and ordained you that ye should go and bring forth fruit, and that your fruit should remain." John says of Christ, We love him because he first loved us. If David had occasion, as the son of Jesse the Bethlehemite, to say, in wonder at God's covenant promises to him, "Who am I, O Lord God, and what is my house, that thou hast brought me hitherto?" surely the fishermen of Galilee, and Matthew the publican, might exclaim, with, at least, equal wonder and humility, "Not unto us, O Lord, not unto us, but unto thy name give glory, for thy mercy, and for thy truth's sake."

Here were two men, Andrew and Peter, busy at their work, spreading their net in the sea. They had already seen Him of whom Moses in the law and the prophets did write; and now, as they plied their task as fishermen, perhaps they talked together of Him whom kings and prophets had desired to see, but had not seen him, while these two fishermen had seen where he dwelt and had abode with him for a part of a day. They were brothers. They were kind brothers. The first thing which Andrew did, when John the Baptist pointed out Christ to him, was, to find his own brother Simon. No family quarrel, or small jealousy, or alienated affection, severed them; but Andrew brought his brother, Simon, to Jesus; and now, as they go back to their lake and their nets, behold, how good and pleasant they find it for brethren to dwell together in unity. Jesus called them as brothers, and blessed them as brothers. As they cast out their net together into the lake, intent only on the shoal of fishes which they see, or expect, in that place, a voice behind them, from the shore, speaks, "Come ye after me, and I will make you fishers of men." It is their new Friend. Some irresistible influence accompanied the word; "and straightway they forsook their nets, and followed him. And when he had gone a little farther thence, he saw James, the son of Zebedee, and John, his brother, who also were in the ship, mending their nets," with their father and hired servants. The busy group, at work on their fishing tackle, lifted up their heads at the sound of a strange, but wonder-working voice, directed to those two brothers, commanding them to follow. And they left their father, Zebedee, in the ship, with the hired servants, and went after him. Two brothers, again, coming together to Christ, to spend life and eternity together, in his service. In the last chapter of John, we read of Judas, the brother of James, and, turning to the Epistle of this Judas, or Jude, we also read, 'Jude, the servant of Christ, and brother of James.' Three pairs of brothers, then, among the first twelve apostles. Brothers, Christ has consecrated your relationship. He loves to have brothers joined in his service.

There is another apostle, still, whom Christ must find, and for that purpose he would go forth into Galilee, and findeth Philip, and saith unto him, Follow me. What condescension and kindness, to go after him, as though he were a personage of importance.

Again: he passes by the place where the customs, or taxes, are payable; a man sits there, with his parchments and writing materials around him, and Christ says to him, Follow me. And he arose, and followed him.

O Saviour, the prophecy is fulfilled in thee: "I am sought of them that asked not for me, I am found of them that sought me not; I said, Behold me, behold me, unto a nation that was not called by my name." Behold, thus thou 'shalt call a nation which thou knewest not, and nations that knew not thee shall run unto thee.'

There is no one of us, Christian brethren and friends, who is not, in like manner, an instance of sovereign, selecting mercy. Never, while memory remains, can you cease to say,

> "Jesus sought me when a stranger,
> Wandering from the fold of God."

With all the distinctness and separateness with which Christ called Andrew, and Peter, and Philip, and Matthew, did he fix his thoughts on you, and call you. He came "to seek and to save" you. There was a time when, at your work, or in your travels, or in your home, or in your pew, or on the deep; sick, bereaved, or rejoicing in some great blessing, Christ stood, and said to you, Follow me; and you arose and followed him. See, in the calling of these men, how Christ has treated you; and be prepared, by adoring thoughts of his sovereign love, to cast your crowns, with the apostles, at his feet, saying, "And hath made us kings and priests unto God and his Father." What humility it should excite in us; how destitute of pride, and haughtiness, and coldness, and repulsiveness, how meek, and gentle, and affable, as Christians, we ought to be, to think that, if we are Christians, it is of pure grace, mercy to the undeserving, the voluntary search of the good Shepherd after sheep that had wandered, and had loved to wander.

III. Christ, in his selection of the apostles, teaches us, that the kingdom of heaven belongs to the poor in spirit.

These men had no ambitious, aspiring thoughts, such as learning, and riches, and rank, and talents too often excite. Passing by, that very morning, perhaps, the place where the sanhedrim were in session, or the scribes and Pharisees, and all the doctors of the law, were gathering together, — neglecting, too, the whole priesthood, — Jesus goes to some obscure men, poor in spirit, and makes them rulers over all that he had.

It is a great satisfaction, when God calls us to any promotion, whether of happiness or honor, to reflect that we had not been laying ambitious plans for it, but were meekly and patiently following our humble business, or our appointed work, whatever it may have been; and that he, in his own good time, called us to inherit and to serve in the place which he had chosen for us. Even if we have been so unwise as to hasten the events of Providence, in any thing upon which we had set our hearts, we have found, afterwards, that God's time and plan were the best, and, if patience had had her perfect work, our satisfaction in his allotments would have been more perfect. That is the best honor and happiness, to which God calls a man when he is not expecting it, but is contentedly doing his duty, as unto God and not unto men, in the place which Providence had assigned him. In like manner, if we but feel our unworthiness, and that the least of God's mercies is more than we merit, and when he afflicts us, that it is far less than we deserve, we shall be sure to receive great spiritual blessings. The reason why many a man is not converted is, he is lofty, and self-sufficient, and feels that he is rich, and in need of nothing. So he sits in judgment on the doctrines and word of God, and rejects all which does not please his fancy, and disdains to come as a humble inquirer, and ask, What must I do to be saved? The fishermen and the publican go into the kingdom of heaven, and become great there, while the proud Pharisee stalks by, blows his trumpet, gives alms, kneels at the corner of the street to say his prayers, and goes to the council, where Jesus stands arraigned, and cries, Crucify him, crucify him. Let us be sure of this, as we see how Christ began to gather together his disciples and apostles, that many things which are highly esteemed among men are abomination in the sight of God; and that 'whoso doth not receive the kingdom of God as a little child shall in no wise enter therein.'

We are to feel encouraged, also, as we see our calling, how that not many wise, not many mighty, not many noble, are called. The kingdom of Christ is like a free republic, in which any citizen, without distinction, may be admitted to the highest privileges and honors. How unlike the spirit of tyrannical lords spiritual, and the systems of ecclesiastical prerogatives. God will take a man from the sheepfold and make him the progenitor of the Messiah, who, while he is David's Lord, shall be David's son.

When that Messiah sets up his kingdom, he will turn away from the seats of learning for his first apostles, and go down to the beach among the fishing boats, and four men in their fishing garb, with their nets in their hand, shall hear his voice, and follow him. "Blessed are ye poor, for yours is the kingdom of God."

Our learning, and cultivation, and wealth, and honors are nothing to Christ. "He poureth contempt upon princes, and raiseth the poor out of the dunghill." So that if we would enter the kingdom of heaven, while we need not change our condition in life, we must have the temper and spirit of the humble poor; for 'to this man God will look, even to him who is poor and of a contrite spirit, and trembleth at his word.'

IV. The promptness with which the apostles forsook all for Christ, teaches us how we should obey his call.

We have all been called by him. He is calling some of us now. See how these men responded, when Jesus said to them, as he now says to some of us, Follow me. Andrew and Peter left their nets and followed him. Some of us, there is reason to fear, would have said, Lord, suffer us first to enclose this draught of fishes. We are poor. We need to labor diligently for our livelihood. James and John, had they felt like some of us, would have said to their father, What shall we do? Matthew the publican would have pleaded his pressing business.

There is something — shall we call it sublime, or beautiful? — in the way in which those men obeyed Christ. Half the merit of obedience consists in promptness. A lingering, hesitating child never satisfies a parent's wishes and feelings; but, "Here am I; send me," always awakens love. The conduct of many with regard to their religious feelings and practice, reminds one of Solomon's exclamation: "As vinegar to the teeth and as smoke to the eyes, so is a sluggard to them that send him." The wise man seems to have had a great repugnance to sluggards. Dilatoriness, want of punctuality, in one employed to serve you, is a trial. The Laodicean church, by its indifference in religion, excited the peculiar reprehension of Christ. There is nothing more suitable than an immediate compliance with the first call which Christ makes. To hesitate, to question, to be afraid, how unworthy all this is of Christ, and of the infinite blessedness of that service to which he calls men. It is a wonder of mercy that he ever calls us a second time; that he "will wait to be gracious." These apostles forsook every thing, risked every thing, to follow Christ. They did not sit in their boats, feeling the pulse of their affections, questioning if they really loved Christ, or if they should persevere in serving him, thinking how bad it would be to follow Christ a while and then falter; but they rose up and followed him; and that effort, and that full committal of their all to him, were the means, by his grace, of securing their affections and obedience. The whole cause of sluggishness in coming to Christ is, a want of proper confidence in him, an unwillingness or fear to commit ourselves to him. If any man ever had reason to hesitate about following Christ, it was Peter. He knew how prone he was to waver in his feelings, how inconstant his affections; and though bold as a lion sometimes, yet, as the king of beasts is said to tremble at the crowing of the cock, so Peter was easily shaken; and he was the last man, knowing his own heart, who, we should have supposed, would have ventured to follow Christ. But he said to the Saviour, "Lo, we have left all, and have followed thee." What was the consequence? He did falter. His faith sometimes failed him. He undertakes to walk on the water to Christ, and sinks, and cries for help. He follows Christ afar off at the time of the Saviour's arrest. He denies him with oaths and cursing. But Christ has prayed for him, that his faith fail not, and he becomes, at last, that which Christ surnamed him, a rock; He built his church on him, as one of the foundations, and the gates of hell have never prevailed against it. And now the walls of that emblematical heavenly city bear, in the foundations of jasper, emerald, and sapphire, the name of Simon Peter, the man who did not stop to think, when Christ called him, Shall I persevere ? but threw himself at the Saviour's feet, and found him able to keep that which he had committed unto him against that day. We, who profess to have followed Christ, sometimes wish that we could, with our present knowledge and experience, have the opportunity again to obey the first call of Christ. We would have you improve upon our backwardness, and be admonished by our error; and we, as Christians, would follow Christ now in such a way as to show to you, and to all, that we, too, have forsaken all to follow him.

V. THE HISTORY OF THE APOSTLES TEACHES US THE REWARDS WHICH CHRIST GIVES HIS FAITHFUL SERVANTS.

No one ever served him for nothing. If he requires much of us, he gives more. "He that loveth son and daughter more than me is not worthy of me." "If any man come after me, and forsake not all that he hath, he cannot be my disciple." 'If any man hate not his own life also, he cannot be my disciple.' Such are his requisitions. What did he give these followers to recompense them for their self-sacrifice ? In the first place, The pleasure they had in doing it was reward enough. But, in the second place, They enjoyed the richest of blessings. They had the Saviour's constant instructions. They enjoyed his constant watch and care. 'Those whom thou hast given me I have kept.' 'While I was in the world I kept them in thy name.' They enjoyed his love. 'Having loved his own which were in the world, he loved them unto the end.' He bestowed great favors upon them. Three of them went to the mount of transfiguration with him, and, though they were sore afraid, the remembrance of it, afterward, was inexpressibly interesting to them. They went with him, also, unto Gethsemane; and though they slept there, yet the recollection of such friendship, in making them companions in his sore distress, afterward bound them to his cause with bonds which were stronger than death. He took them with him to Olivet; prayed with them; gave them their commission to go into all the world, and preach the gospel to every creature; endowed them with miraculous gifts; and went up to heaven in their sight, promising still to be with them alway, even unto the end of the world. They received the Holy Ghost and the gift of tongues. They spread the knowledge of his name to the ends of the earth. Two of them wrote the most important of the four Gospels; and four of them, Epistles, which are guiding generations of men to heaven; and one of them was employed to reveal heaven itself to men. Thus we see with what appropriateness their names are symbolically represented to us as inscribed in the foundation stones of heaven, because they were honored with the work of building up the kingdom of Christ from its foundations; and all who are saved are said to be built on the foundation of the apostles and prophets, Jesus Christ himself being the chief corner stone.

What though the most of them died by martyrdom? They rejoiced that they were counted worthy to suffer. When Peter came to be crucified, he only requested to die with his head downward, as not worthy to suffer like his Master. Their pains were sharp, but they were short; and the end was life everlasting. What must be the reflections of those men in heaven. Some of them look back to that Lake of Galilee; they think of that moment when Christ called them. Matthew recollects his seat at the customs — how Christ came by and said, "Follow me;" and from the moment of their prompt obedience they date the beginning of their blissful eternity. Had one of us, perhaps they say, had one of us hesitated to follow Christ; had we loved the world; had we been afraid to commit our all to Christ; or had we feared that we should not hold out, and so had not set out, — what should we have lost. Where in the universe is there wealth enough, honor enough, bliss enough, to make one of them willing that his emblazoned name should be rased from that foundation stone? Where else in the universe would they give one poor thought or wish to have it recorded? All this is the consequence of that which is written in this brief verse: "And Jesus said unto him, Follow me. And he arose, and followed him."

When Christ calls us, we know not what he intends to do by us and with us. Would we but give ourselves up to him at once, with cheerfulness and entire confidence, thinking not of our weakness and unworthiness, but of his power and faithfulness, he might employ us to glorify him; and thus identify our names with that kingdom which is to be eternal.

When you think of what these men did in the brief period of their lives, and what the consequences were and will be, what an imperishable happiness they have secured for themselves, what glory and honor will forever belong to their names, and then consider that Christ calls us to be his servants, telling us that, if we be faithful over few things, he will make us rulers over many things, and then reflect how fast life passes away, how much of it is gone with many, how earnest and laborious they must be if they would answer life's great end, it would seem that every one would respond to the first call of his God and Saviour, and, without delay, consecrate himself to Christ, who calls him to his eternal kingdom and glory. What if we fail at last to have a place within that heavenly city, where the fruits of the gospel are gathered from this world? Where shall we be, if not included in those walls whose foundations are sealed with the names of the apostles of the Lamb?

VI. The name of Judas stands in affecting contrast to the names of the apostles.

Good were it for that man, the Saviour said, if he had never been born. Of course he will not, even after the lapse of ages, be received to heaven; for then an eternity of happiness would compensate for all that he had suffered. He has gone to his own place. His name is covered with eternal infamy. So long as redemption is remembered, so long as Jesus reigns in glory, and the Lamb is the light of heaven, so long the name and history of Judas will be remembered for shame and everlasting contempt. The names of the other apostles grace the foundations of heaven; those precious stones are a shrine to their names, themselves more precious than rubies. His name is on the walls of hell, and his deeds are covered with the blackness of darkness forever.

How true it is that whoever has any thing to do with Christ, whoever is distinguished at all by the Saviour's favor, whoever has his name coupled, for good or ill, with the cause of Christ, is raised by it to a proud distinction or to a bad eminence, according to his deeds. To be a friend of Christ is glory and honor; and this in proportion to the ardor and constancy of your love. To be an enemy to Christ, or, in other words, not to be his friend, is to have our portion with the lost, in sufferings and sorrows proportionate to our opportunities of knowing, loving, and serving Christ.

Those days, when Jesus walked and talked with him, ate with him, and even kneeled to wash his feet, occur to the unhappy Judas, as the day of grace with him, when he, too, might have had his name written with the rest of the apostles in the foundations of heaven. There is no vacant place in those walls marked with outlines of sable stone, no mourning tablet, where the name of Judas should have been, and testifying sorrow at his loss. The place of his name is filled with that of another. So, "If thou art wise, thou art wise for thyself, and if thou scornest, thou alone shalt bear it." Christ offers you a place in glory, and, what is, surely, an additional honor and privilege, if you can believe it, a place in his church here, and an apostleship to your fellow-men, and then a place in heaven, where you shall see and enjoy the fruit of your labor. But, if you refuse, there are others that will take that which you reject. And you will be left to think, What did I gain by rejecting Christ and religion? Perhaps as much, and perhaps not so much, as Judas gained in exchange for his apostleship, his Christian character, his interest in Christ, his inheritance in heaven. Thus it may be with you. Some bawble, some idolatrous desire for show or pleasure, some lust, some secret shame, or sloth, is the price for which many are parting with Christ, and their eternal all; and some of them are members of Christ's church. You will lose even the price of your iniquity, which will perish with the using, or be taken from you at death. Those thirty pieces of silver were flung down, and flung away, upon the stone floor of the temple. O sinner, you are bartering heaven, selling Christ, putting your soul into the hands of Satan, in exchange for that which will soon seem to be nothing. False professors, you are preparing for an eternity with Judas, going from the company of Christ's disciples to your own place. Ye friends of Christ, not in name only, but in deed and truth his friends, hear his promise: "He that confesseth me before men, him will I also confess before my Father, and before his angels." "Ye are they that have continued with me in my temptations, and I appoint unto you a kingdom, as my Father hath appointed unto me, that ye may eat and drink at my table, and sit on thrones, judging the twelve tribes of Israel." Are Andrew, and Peter, and Matthew, and Philip, raised from obscurity, by being each a devoted friend to Jesus? So shall it be with you, if you live for Christ. "And behold, there are last that shall be first." Consecrate yourselves to him. Do it with a promptness, with a confidence in him, with an entireness, which shall testify for you in the day of his appearing. Simon Peter appeals to us, with the true motive, and the great reward:—"THAT, WHEN HIS GLORY SHALL BE REVEALED, YE MAY BE GLAD ALSO, WITH EXCEEDING JOY."

SERMON VI.

THE CHILDREN IN THE TEMPLE.

MATTHEW XXI. 15.

HOSANNA TO THE SON OF DAVID.

The obligations of children to the Saviour of the world are peculiar, and deeply interesting. We should expect to find some demonstration from them to their infinite Friend, among the testimonials of love and worship given to him during his earthly life.

Their hosanna, in the temple, is a part of a most interesting passage in the Saviour's history, which we must attentively consider, to understand the children's worship.

One of the most affecting things connected with the Saviour's sufferings and death, is, the zeal with which he hastened to suffer, at the time appointed. "And they were in the way going up to Jerusalem; and Jesus went before them, and they were amazed." The disciples knew that this was his last journey to Jerusalem, where he was to be crucified; and yet there was an earnestness in his manner, at which, as the evangelist says, the companions of his journey 'were amazed.' He passed on at some distance before them, leaving them behind, in his apparent zeal to reach the city. Supernatural impressions seemed to be upon him, making his whole appearance somewhat strange and marvellous, whereupon he repeated the information already given: "Behold, we go up to Jerusalem, and the Son of man shall be delivered unto the chief priests and scribes, and they shall condemn him to death, and shall deliver him to the Gentiles, and they shall mock him, and shall scourge him, and shall spit upon him, and shall kill him; and the third day he shall rise again." In full knowledge of all this, he hasted to the place of sacrifice, fulfilling his own words respecting the yielding up of his life: "No man taketh it from me, but I lay it down of myself; I have power to lay it down, and I have power to take it again." Thus we see him "pouring out his soul unto death, and making intercession for the transgressors."

Arriving at Bethphage, which was a village whose site has perished, but near Bethany, and between two and three miles from Jerusalem, he paused before he entered the great city. He was never to leave the place again till he left it for heaven, except as he retired at night to Bethany, to sleep.

He prepared for his entrance into Jerusalem in a

remarkable manner. Instead of passing into the city as usual, like a worn and weary traveller, undistinguished from the multitude, and unnoticed, he proposes to make a sort of triumphal entry. It was the only instance of the kind, in his history, in which he departed from the plain and ordinary methods of common life; but, now, he will manifest himself, not as a man of sorrows, but as King of Zion. When the time had come for him to suffer and die, you remember that he said, "Now is the Son of man glorified"; therefore, when he entered the city to die, he entered it as a king. It is plain that Christ regarded his death as the grand event of his coming into the world. It was not, principally, to be a teacher, nor an example; he is the 'Lamb of God'; he came to make a sacrifice "of his body, once for all," "to give his life a ransom for many." When the time to do this arrives, he begins to assume the character of a king; and it was only when he came to die, that he assumed to be a king. Death was his coronation. The reed for a sceptre, the purple robe, the bowing of the knee before him, Pilate's inscription on the cross, 'This is the King of the Jews,' were all truly significant of his kingly character, though his enemies meant them for mockery. In passing to the altar of sacrifice, Jesus goes triumphantly as king.

Now, we will look at this King as he passes by.

We know that he is "the Prince of the kings of the earth." He is to "reign till all enemies are put under his feet." He is to have upon his head "many crowns." He is to see the whole earth at his feet, and the hosts of heaven. Jerusalem, as the metropolis of the church of God, and representing the seat of his spiritual government, is now to be entered by him in his royal capacity; but, strange to say, he enters there to reach his kingdom and ascend his throne by suffering and dying on a cross, between two thieves.

He directed two of his disciples to bring him a young ass, with her colt; and that colt, whereon never man sat, was chosen by him to ride upon into Jerusalem.

They who think that there was something low or mean in this, are wholly mistaken. The general use of the horse was prohibited to the Jews, because it excited a reliance upon outward means of defence in war, to the neglect of immediate help from God. The ass was not held in such contempt as in countries where the horse is common. Deborah thus addressès the governors of Israel, as those 'that ride upon white asses.' David rode upon a mule, and directed that Solomon should do the same at his coronation.

So that all which was remarkable in what Christ did on this occasion was, that He, who is Lord of lords and King of kings, should ride like other men; which was literally the case, if we except two or three things, in this instance, which indicate humility, but nothing affected, and nothing mean. One is, that he had no animal of his own; for he "had not where to lay his head." He borrowed either of one who was a friend, or, by his almighty power, inclined the heart of the owner, a stranger, to lend to him. Another is, that he made no show of ornament or rank. They brought no Roman saddle, with housing of purple and gold, nor curious bridle; but just as a man in those days would ride, with the halter or string, which tied the animal, and merely his own loose upper garment thrown upon the creature's back, with nothing to attract notice, just as John would have rode, or Philip, so Jesus rode toward the city of the great King.

And now, though, as before observed, there was nothing mean or affected in this, we perceive in it wonderful meekness and condescension. True, it is all in keeping with the history of Him who was laid in the manger. Why did he enter Jerusalem in this manner? We are expressly informed upon this question. "All this was done, that it might be fulfilled which was spoken by the prophet, saying, Tell ye the daughter of Zion, Behold, thy King cometh unto thee, meek, and sitting upon an ass, and a colt, the foal of an ass." We find this prophecy in

Zechariah: "Rejoice greatly, O daughter of Zion; shout, O daughter of Jerusalem; behold, thy King cometh unto thee; he is just, and having salvation; lowly, and riding upon an ass, and upon a colt, the foal of an ass."

The kings of the earth, in those days, would have come with horses, and chariots, and bands of music; with a body guard, and a great retinue. The King of heaven proceeds to his throne in humble mien; and, when they saw him, there was 'no beauty in him, that they should desire him.' He wished to make men see that, in all his feelings and sympathies, he was one of them, and to be able, with the powerful proof of a consistent life, to say, "Take my yoke upon you, and learn of me, for I am meek and lowly in heart, and ye shall find rest unto your souls." But the full meaning of this humble entrance into Jerusalem did not appear to the disciples at the time, as one of them, the evangelist John, tells us: "These things understood not his disciples at the first; but, when Jesus was glorified, then remembered they that these things were written of him, and that they had done these things unto him." How they must have wondered when they saw him pouring out his Spirit, and converting the tribes of the earth; how John, in Patmos, must have wondered, when he saw him on the throne of the universe; how we shall wonder, when we see him coming in the clouds of heaven, and all his holy angels with him, to think that, when he entered Jerusalem to suffer and die, nay, in his kingly character, taking the last step from the cross to his universal throne, he should have rode upon that humble beast, with Simon Peter's garment, it may be, or Iscariot's, thrown upon the creature, with no regard to style or attractiveness in his manner. Our hearts bow before this great God and Saviour; our pride is hateful, and our vanity is sickening. Are we offended at the thought of such a Saviour? "Blessed is he," Christ said, "whosoever shall not be offended in me."

This entrance of Christ was, nevertheless, a triumph, as will now appear.

It was the week of the Passover. Jerusalem was filled with people from all parts of the land, and this time was chosen for this triumphal, emblematical coming of the King of Zion. It was a preternatural influence that moved the multitude of the disciples, just at that time, to do honor to Christ. As soon as Christ began to ride, the whole population around him seemed to be moved by an impulse as sudden as when a rising wind shakes the tree tops, and the woods begin to rustle, and bend before the breeze. Why the multitude of disciples should have been affected in this manner, just at this time, you cannot explain, except as you attribute it to the special power of God. It was like some revivals of religion, — the sudden, special presence of God's Spirit, that heavenly wind, blowing where it listeth. For we read, "And a very great multitude spread their garments in the way; others cut down branches from the trees, and strewed them in the way." Like a popular enthusiasm, as when a multitude detach the horses from the chariot of a distinguished guest, and draw it themselves in triumph, and others strew flowers and garlands along the road, so, in this strange and sudden demonstration, the multitude that were attracted by the news that Christ was on his way to Jerusalem, threw down their garments for this King, while others gathered branches from the trees, and made the path before him green. "And the multitudes that went before, and that followed, cried, saying, Hosanna to the Son of David: blessed is he that cometh in the name of the Lord; hosanna in the highest." John says, "The people, therefore, that was with him when he called Lazarus out of his grave, and raised him from the dead, bear record. For this cause the people also met him; for that they heard that he had done this miracle." "And when he was come into Jerusalem, all the city was moved, saying, Who is this?" We may answer them, and say, What is this? He has been daily with you in the temple, and ye never cried, Hosanna, in this manner, nor gave him such a triumphal reception.

We see in all this that wonderful stream, that under current, of prophetic events, bearing forward the great mysteries of the kingdom of heaven, the day of days, when Moses and Aaron, and the prophets, altars and visions, are all to be superseded, being fulfilled, by the great atoning sacrifice of the Lamb of God. John afterward in vision said, "And I looked, and lo, a Lamb stood on the Mount Zion, and with him a hundred and forty and four thousand, having his Father's name written in their foreheads. And I heard a voice from heaven as the voice of many waters, and as the voice of a great thunder, and I heard the voice of harpers harping with their harps." The 'Lamb' was now on his way to the earthly 'Mount Zion'; thence he goes to Calvary, and thence to Mount Zion above, where, as Redeemer, he is to be loved and worshipped.

How easy it is for God to move the hearts of men to fulfil his purposes. "Thy people shall be willing in the day of thy power." Christ must receive the acclamations of the people now, and ride prosperously into the great city of David, as an emblem of his coming ascendency over the house of David, as well as over the Gentiles. But let us follow this triumphant King. Whither does he lead us? Surely to the palace, where he will proclaim his kingdom; or to some high place, where he will summon the world to do him homage. Instead of this, he moves directly to the temple. There, what a sight do we behold. The vacant spaces have been seized upon by traffickers in articles for sacrifice, and by men who changed foreign coin into current money, and large sums into half shekels, which were demanded in religious tribute. The near approach of the passover, with its sacrifices and offerings, made the temple like a market house before some great festival, and sheep, and oxen, and doves for sale, crowded out all appearance of devotion. These traders he cast out of the temple, and overthrew the tables of the money changers, spilling their coins on the floor, and turning over the seats of those that sold doves. All this he had done once before, at the first passover which occurred after his public ministry began, when he made a scourge of small cords, and put the whole crew of them to flight, with their sheep and cattle. The fourth and last passover during his life has come, and he again vindicates God's house from its abuses, and having cleared the place, he begins his works of mercy there. "And the blind and the lame came to him in the temple, and he healed them."

Then all they that were waiting for the consolation of Israel were glad, and there was great joy in that city. Many a humble, yet strong believer triumphed, that day, at the thought of his meek and lowly Saviour riding, as he did, into the great city, and there purging the temple, and manifesting forth his glory as the benefactor of the poor, the Saviour of the broken-hearted, the friend of sinners. We can fancy that we hear voluntary choirs of them singing praises, in the words of one of the Psalms: "In Judah is God known, his name is great in Israel. In Salem also is his tabernacle, and his dwelling-place in Zion. There brake he the arrows of the bow, the shield, and the sword, and the battle. Thou art more glorious and excellent than the mountains of prey. At thy rebuke, O God of Jacob, both the chariot and the horse are cast into a dead sleep. Thou, even thou, art to be feared; and who may stand in thy sight when once thou art angry? Thou didst cause judgment to be heard from heaven; the earth feared and was still, when God arose to judgment, to save all the meek of the earth. Surely the wrath of man shall praise thee; the remainder of wrath shalt thou restrain. Vow, and pay unto the Lord your God; let all that be round about him bring presents unto him that ought to be feared. He shall cut off the spirit of princes; he is terrible to the kings of the earth."

Probably this was, to many, the happiest hour, thus far, of their lives. Christ had manifested forth his glory; Zechariah's vision was fulfilled, and his exhortation was obeyed: "Rejoice greatly, O daughter of Zion, shout, O daughter of Jerusalem; behold thy King cometh to thee; he is just and having salvation." Well might they rejoice, to see him clothing himself with majesty, and reforming abuses which had made their hearts burn with indignation. We love bold, strong measures in reforming great abuses, in opposing wicked and violent men; and the moral courage and the energetic arm which are adequate for such emergencies, are regarded by us with a veneration and love not far from worship. But when he who, in this superhuman manner, had scattered these traders, and their sheep, and oxen, and doves, and money, proceeded, with condescending kindness, to heal the blind and the lame, joy and praise were without bounds.

There were some striking and deeply-interesting sounds in those shouts of praise. Children, who had been brought to the temple by their devout parents, or who had resorted thither as a place of public gathering, began to sing, "Hosanna to the Son of David." Their demonstration of joy was so conspicuous amid the whole scene of triumph, that the chief priests and scribes had their attention attracted by it, and they were sore displeased. They appealed to Christ, saying, 'Hearest thou what these say,' these young idolaters, offering divine worship in a senseless manner, knowing nothing of what their words import? 'Hearest thou what these say?' "And Jesus saith unto them, Yea, have ye never read, Out of the mouths of babes and sucklings thou hast perfected praise?" He did not finish the passage, but left it to them to supply the words, "that thou mightest still the enemy and the avenger."

This choir of young voices must be regarded as a part of the whole scene of triumph and joy, which we have considered at length as forming the background to this more conspicuous group, which attracted the notice of the envious and angry priests and scribes. It was ordered that the children should bear a part in the Saviour's triumph, that the children should swell the praises of Zion's King, welcoming him, and cheering his spirit as he came to the last, awful scenes of suffering and death.

Amidst the praises of the children in the temple, we see him, according to Jacob's dying words concerning him, "binding his foal to the vine, and his ass's colt to the choice vine; he washed his garments in wine, and his clothes in the blood of grapes."

Should a multitude of children, on a public occasion, be seized with an enthusiasm in favor of some personage, the more that it seemed suggested by no obvious cause, the more would it have the effect of a supernatural impulse directly imparted to them; for, in popular commotions, a crowd of women and children, borne forward by their excited feelings, are far more irresistible than so many men. Bayonets and swords lose their power in such a presence. Attention is forcibly drawn to them. Their enthusiastic actions and words strike harshly upon the feelings of the churlish and irritable among the spectators, who are not in sympathy with the occasion.

This sudden impulse upon the minds of the children, in praising Christ, must have had a grateful effect upon his feelings, considering the near approach of his sufferings and death; and their love, at such a time, is, perhaps, a fulfilment of another prophecy concerning him: "He shall drink of the brook by the way; therefore shall he lift up the head;" that is, as he goes to suffer and die, his spirits shall be cheered by manifestations of love, which are like unexpected brooks to a weary traveller. The alabaster box of ointment was another brook; the angel in Gethsemane was another; and the great company of women, following him to Calvary, and lamenting him, was another.

Some may say, 'This act of the children in the temple was a mere childish and thoughtless thing. Children are great imitators. No account is to be made of their hosanna.' Christ did not think so. He considered it as an offering made to him, and quoted Scripture to explain and justify it. Is it the spirit of the scribes and Pharisees within us, that leads us to think lightly of the children's hosanna?

It is easy to show cause why children should have been moved with interest in the triumph of Christ, and should have joined to love and worship him.

Perhaps it is safe to assert that

THERE IS NO CLASS OF THE HUMAN RACE WHICH, AS A CLASS, IS UNDER SUCH OBLIGATIONS TO CHRIST AS YOUNG CHILDREN.

It is probable that Christ has saved the souls of more young children than of grown persons. It is estimated that more than two thirds of all who are born, die in infancy and early childhood. We have reason to hope and believe that they who are incapable of repentance and faith, though partakers of a corrupt nature through Adam, share in the benefits of redemption by Christ; so that, where sin abounded, grace doth much more abound. Some insist that children are saved because it would be injustice to them if they should be lost. With such feelings, we should have said, beforehand, that it would be unjust that children should suffer in this world for the vices and crimes of their parents, as they do. We must not put the salvation of infants and children on the ground of any thing due to them; nor should we sit in judgment on the question, What is God bound in justice to do? Should he, in his holy and wise decrees, have ordained that the child of every enemy of his should perish with the wicked parent, we should, perhaps, only have said, 'How unsearchable are his judgments, and his ways past finding out.' Some are far too ready to say what God should do and what he should not do, who might, with profit to themselves, have such a vision as Eliphaz, the friend of Job, had, when a spirit passed before his face, and the hair of his flesh stood up. "It stood still, and there was silence; and I heard a voice, saying, Shall mortal man be more just than God? Shall a man be more pure than his Maker? Behold, he put no trust in his servants, and his angels he charged with folly. How much less in them that dwell in houses of clay, whose foundation is the dust, and which are crushed before the moth."

While the Bible is silent on the subject, there is reason to hope and to believe that God has glorified himself by saving the myriads of children who have perished by disease, war, famine, infanticide. Salvation being, in every case, an act of grace, grace is especially honored in rescuing the poor, wretched heirs of sin, who die in early years, and making them the subjects of Christ's redeeming work, — they being renewed by the Holy Ghost, and thus made the fruits of the Saviour's death. Unless they are saved in this way, there will be a majority in heaven who will not sing the song of heaven, "Unto him that loved us, and washed us from our sins in his own blood." That vast multitude would then say, We owe it to the justice of God, — it is something which God was obliged in justice to bestow on us, that we are here. John saw and heard nothing like this in heaven. Now, if young children are saved by Christ, if they owe heaven to his death, of course they needed redemption, on account of their being involved in the fall. If it would have been unjust to punish them for Adam's sin, it does not follow that their being saved is not an act of grace. Their rescue from all liability to perish, by actual transgression, had they lived, is enough to lay them under infinite obligations to Christ. An old epitaph reads thus:

> "Bold Infidelity, turn pale and die;
> Beneath this stone four infants' ashes lie.
> Say, are they lost or saved?
> If death's by sin, they sinned,—for they lie here;
> If heaven's by works, in heaven they can't appear.
> Reason, ah, how depraved; revere the sacred page;
> They died, for Adam sinned; they live, for Jesus died."

It is interesting to think, that of all who have, thus far, been saved, the majority are children. Think of the great proportion who die in childhood, in Christian lands. Then think of lands and of generations from which very few adults have gone to heaven, and you see how children have multiplied the numbers of the redeemed. When Christ said, 'Suffer the little children to come unto me, and forbid them not, for of such is the kingdom of God,' no doubt he meant to say, These, also, are included in the offers and intentions of the gospel. And when he saw children, it must have reminded him of his home in heaven, where

"Millions of infant souls compose
The family above."

He had always known, that, of all the souls who arrive at heaven's gate, the vast majority are children; and he might also have implied, The kingdom of God is composed, in the larger proportion, of such.

To those of our race who go to heaven in adult years, this large admixture of children in the society of heaven must be inexpressibly pleasant. There are no scribes and Pharisees there; no temper morose and sour, to be offended by children. There is sufficient age and maturity there, to redeem the society of heaven from an infantile character, even if the children remained children; but what freshness and beauty the sight, the joy, the voices of the young in heaven must impart to that world. If "a child in a house is a well-spring of pleasure," and if childhood in heaven rejoices the hearts of men and women as it does on earth, there must be joy unspeakable there. Christ warned his disciples not to despise a child, for the reason that the angels, who minister to them, are 'presence angels'; "for I say unto you, their angels do always behold the face of my Father which is in heaven." It must be to Christ a sight of inexpressible love and satisfaction, as he sees these millions on millions redeemed from their helpless state of sin and ruin. What is their song? Surely this: 'Not by works of righteousness which we had done, but of his mercy he saved us, by the washing of regeneration, and the renewing of the Holy Ghost, which he shed on us abundantly, through Jesus Christ our Saviour.' As each feeble spirit of an infant, and of a young child, comes up from earth, there must be unutterable tenderness and love toward it on the part of many there, knowing, as they do, what weeping and lamentation, in many cases, the little spirit has left in the household; there must be joy over it, to think of its early escape from a world of sin; and, in some cases, there must be an exultation which, perhaps, would seem strange to us; and that is, when a child arrives from a family where one or both the parents are not the friends of God. Sweet child, you can no more have your salvation perilled by a prayerless, godless father. The mother that bare you never said, "For this child I prayed," nor consecrated you to your Maker and Redeemer; nor, had you lived, would she have thought of any thing else for you than the world, and sinful or transitory joys. God set his love on you; the prayers of some pious ancestor, perhaps, have been for a memorial before God, and he determined that, at least, one of that family should be saved. Welcome, welcome to this place of safety; welcome from the dangers of a prayerless house. "Is not this a brand plucked out of the fire?"

What is more interesting than the opening mind of a child, when the world begins to break in upon it, and wonder and delight are felt at every new discovery? What must it be to contemplate the joy of those souls as heaven breaks in upon their senses? Every spirit that enters heaven is, in some sense, like a child, amid those new and strange scenes; and so was every new-born angel; they remember their first impressions always, and it gives them the deeper interest in those whose tender age makes slower progress in the conceptions of heavenly things. Some anonymous lines on the statuary of "the chanting cherubs" represent the conversation of a child with its guardian angel, on its way from earth to heaven; in which the child says, as it draws near the light which no man can see and live, —

> "O, I cannot bear this glory:
> Sister spirit, how canst thou?"

The angel answers, —

> "I will tell thee all my story;
> I was once as thou art now."

As to the state and the progress of these children in heaven, we know nothing. Saved by grace, as we suppose they are, Jesus receives no crowns laid at his feet, nor listens to any hosannas, more acceptable and pleasing to him than those of the young; in whom he sees the consciousness of peculiar obligations to him, and the greatest illustrations of his love to our ruined race.

If this be so, should not children here on earth, on some occasion, have honored Christ? Had they held their peace, would not the very stones have cried out? They say that there is something in the sea corresponding to every thing on the land — curious and beautiful resemblances to terrestrial things. We love to think that there are correspondences between the kingdom of God on earth and in heaven; and among them we naturally require that the pattern of the heavenly world, in its joys felt and expressed by the young there, should have some counterpart on earth. So, when Christ came to Jerusalem to die, in the temple of God children's voices sung hosannas to the Son of David. What must have been the feelings of children in heaven, acquainted with the work that Christ was doing here on earth, as they saw him hastening to the accursed death of the cross. How they would have flocked around him had they been permitted; how they would have wept with him, and yet how they would have tried to cheer his spirits on the way to the cross, saying, Do not faint ere it is finished. Remember thy family in heaven and on earth, and millions yet unborn; and pay the ransom for us. And so, as they could not themselves sing with audible voices out of heaven to him, these children, their fellow-heirs, — it may be, many of them, of heavenly bliss, — at least their representatives, did it for them, and made such music and such determined adoration, that the angry scribes exclaimed with indignation, "Hearest thou what these say?"

Two practical remarks are naturally suggested by this subject.

I. Children can love and worship Christ.

Many a child in our congregations, who does not think of his duty to love and serve Christ, is old enough to be lost; and if he should die in his present state, we could not think that he is included in the number of those who are saved without repentance and faith because they are incapable of it.

Children that are old enough to sin knowingly, are old enough to repent. If they are old enough to say wicked words, lie, steal, disobey their parents, and quarrel, they are old enough to be punished. As there are very many children in heaven, so there is reason to believe there are many young persons in hell. Those forty and two children who mocked Elisha, it is to be feared, are there, and others like them have perished in their sins. Instead of making excuses for young sinners, always, no doubt God is sometimes peculiarly angry with them, especially if they have pious parents, who have done every thing to make them good. They need a Saviour as much as older people, and must suffer forever, if they die without repenting and accepting Christ. Are any of our children past the age when we could hope for salvation for them without repentance and faith, and are they yet in their sins? Have we been faithful? Are we prepared to stand with them at the judgment seat of Christ? What testimony will those children render before Christ with regard to us?

We should look to see our children converted early. To repeat and enforce a former remark: when some rebuked those that brought children to him, and Christ said, "Of such is the kingdom of God," he undoubtedly meant, I include children in my offers of salvation; my kingdom here on earth is to be made up, in part, of them. It must be acceptable to Christ to have a child love and serve him. We must not limit the power or the grace of Christ, and be displeased at the thought of children being converted. Were we more childlike ourselves, we should be more in sympathy with the experience of children, more wise in our treatment of it, and more successful. As the kingdom of Christ advances, we are to expect that conversions will take place earlier in life. O that we might see, among other signs of the times, this proof that his kingdom is advancing among us — that children are early impressed with their obligations to their Redeemer and Friend. A pastor seldom feels happier than when a child meets him in the street with a joyous face and a kind, respectful greeting. How Christ must love those young friends of his when they go in secret and pray to him, and sing his praise. He said that it would be better that a millstone should be hanged about the neck of any one, and he drowned in the sea, than that he should offend one of these little ones that believe in him.

Some parents greatly err who omit to teach and pray with their children, looking only to the act of conversion to make them religious. While instruction will be useless without a change of heart, the surest way to secure that change for the child is, to surround it with a pious example and every Christian influence; and, besides, its conversion will then be the perfecting of a progressive preparation for intelligent piety, stability, and usefulness. A quaint preacher once said to parents, as an encouragement to instruct their children in the knowledge of God and spiritual things, "Fill the water pots with water, and Christ may turn it into wine." But let us seek and expect the early acknowledgment, by every child, of its obligations to God, and its acceptance of the gospel. What sorrow and misery we may prevent, in ourselves and others, if we are faithful as Christian parents. It is a fearful thing for parents to send forth into society a family of unconverted children

Their last account will be rendered, not with joy, but with grief.

II. Christian parents, if they are faithful, should be encouraged and comforted with regard to their children, in view of the Saviour's power and grace.

Have any of us a child grown beyond our control, disobedient, wicked, a candidate for ruin? While we weep, perhaps, over our sad mistakes or neglect, let us not be discouraged. Pray with the child, again and again; it will help your efforts; it will secure the help of Christ. The creature on which Christ rode in triumph to the place where the children sung hosanna to him, was one on which never man sat. So Christ can break or tame the uncurbed spirit of a son or daughter with infinite ease, and make that child the honored instrument of glorifying him. What steed, with his caparisons of royal wealth, ever bore such a king, or walked in such triumph, as that young, untamed colt which bore Christ so gently amid shouts and over branches thrown down into his path. Let every unbridled, untamed spirit be brought to Christ, with implicit and obedient faith. He can make it willing in the day of his power.

Some of you have representatives among those children whom Christ has gathered into his kingdom.

Could you have seen the reception of your child in heaven, and heard the words that were spoken concerning it, and concerning you, — could you behold it in some circle of the redeemed; the leader of some little choir, or awakening love and wonder at the development of no common power, or the youngest, sweetest singer there; a servant of Christ, doing his commandments, hearkening to the voice of his word; sitting among good men and angels, as Christ sat, at twelve years of age, hearing, and asking questions, — you would cease to weep, except for joy.

What a contrast there is between such a child and you, unconverted parent; for, without doubt, many an unconverted parent has a child in heaven. How much worse than at the dying pillow, and the little grave, will the separation be, when you see the child in the kingdom of God, and you yourself shut out. O miracle of sin; a parent, with a child in heaven, going to hell. Dreadful scenes await us at the judgment seat of Christ. There will be scenes of bliss there, when parents meet their long-lost ones, and find themselves standing in the relation of parents to youthful seraphs, who, in heaven, during these years of parental sorrow, have been growing wise, and excellent in beauty. They will make their parents feel more than old Jacob did, when they told him, 'Joseph is yet alive, and is governor over all Egypt.' Your 'Joseph,' whom they cast into a pit, is yet alive, and sees the face of the King; he thinks of you, and, perhaps, inquires for you, of those who come to heaven, as Joseph did concerning his father. If your bereavement shall be the means of making you a Christian, it will prove that God, in his kind and wise providence, sent the child before you "to preserve life," in the sense of saving your soul.

Have your children ever heard you sing, or repeat, a hymn in praise of Christ, or seen you bow the knee to him? You love your children, and, it may be, idolize them. What if you be bereaved, in the other world, of parental joys; what if you fail to look on that heavenly society, where the young now make it perpetual morning and spring; where children are not unlike flowers and birds to the earth, and where the redemption which was bestowed upon millions of them will pour forth treasures of its love forever, on the happy spirits of the redeemed. Childhood, with some of you, is gone, and Christ had no worship from you. Youth is gone, and the Saviour had no dew of your youth. Ripe years, with you, are falling into the 'sere and yellow leaf,' and you are without Christ. You have a great work to do, and much time to redeem, if you would be found in the number of those who will, at last, appear before Christ, and say, "BEHOLD, I AND THE CHILDREN WHICH GOD HATH GIVEN ME."

SERMON VII.

THE WOMAN WITH THE ALABASTER BOX.

LUKE VII. 37, 38.

AND BEHOLD, A WOMAN IN THE CITY, WHICH WAS A SINNER, WHEN SHE KNEW THAT JESUS SAT AT MEAT IN THE PHARISEE'S HOUSE, BROUGHT AN ALABASTER BOX OF OINTMENT, AND STOOD AT HIS FEET BEHIND HIM, WEEPING, AND BEGAN TO WASH HIS FEET WITH TEARS, AND DID WIPE THEM WITH THE HAIRS OF HER HEAD, AND KISSED HIS FEET, AND ANOINTED THEM WITH THE OINTMENT.

Here is a scene and a transaction, expressing the most intense love, in which not a word is spoken by the principal character. Her feelings were too deep for words. The whole occurrence will appear natural and easy, if we transfer it to our own times.

Suppose that you are sitting at your table, with a company of friends. A stranger glides into the room, with an air of deep grief, earnest, negligent in apparel, yet interesting and striking in her whole appearance. Passing round to one of your guests, and standing behind him, with a look that indicates love blended with sorrow, she bursts into a flood of tears.

If there were any reason to suspect her of insanity, or of a design to insult that guest, or to obtain redress from him by exposing his offences against her to the company, your first impulse would be to have her removed. But if you saw that she was overcome by love and tenderness, and that your guest turned toward her with no forbidding look, but in a way that encouraged her tears, and especially if that guest were a distinguished and good man, for whom you had made that company, your respect for him, and confidence in him, would make you wait in silence to see what he would say and do with regard to that incident, which you would suspect had a meaning and an object, with which you would not feel at liberty to interfere.

We may account, therefore, for the intrusion of this woman into the Pharisee's house at dinner, and his not commanding her to be removed, by making his case our own. He saw that there was some connection between his guest and this stranger, which made it unsuitable for him to interpose. He felt that Christ would treat the stranger in a way becoming the civility and courtesy due to the master of the house. We see his sense of propriety in not making the remark to Christ, but 'within himself': "This man, if he were a prophet, would have known who and what manner of woman this is that toucheth him; for she is a sinner."

We see the Saviour reclining, according to the oriental custom, at the table of a Pharisee, upon the couch; and a woman, impelled by the deepest emotion, entering into the presence of the Pharisee, a stranger to him, unbidden, for the purpose of finding Christ. Let us see what she will do. She stands at the Saviour's feet, as he reclined, with his feet extended, upon the couch; and immediately, as the original has it, she began to rain tears upon his feet. She did not come for that purpose, however. This was an involuntary prelude to her main object. She had something for his feet besides tears; but, as she prepared herself to bestow that other token upon them, her emotions were excited, and the rain descended from her eyes so as to prevent, for a time, her purpose. As fast as her eyes were clouded with her weeping, and overflowed, she wiped the feet on which they fell, with her dishevelled hair, to prepare them for what she had brought. As fast as she dried them thus, they were wet again; till, at length, she grew composed; when, with ardent love and worship, she kissed the feet, and poured on them her alabaster box of ointment. This was a service frequently done to invited guests in the houses of the rich. Their feet were washed to cool them, their heads were anointed with oil, and sometimes their feet were softened and refreshed by anointing them with oil. This woman had bought an alabaster box, filled, not with common oil, but with a prepared ointment She would not pour it upon Christ's head; she was not worthy to touch that head; she went to his feet, and there poured out the gift, which would have been a creditable offering for the richest man to pour upon the head of a guest.

In the Saviour's own words, we have an explanation of this act. "Her sins, which are many, are forgiven; for she loved much." This tells the whole secret of those tears, that kiss, that precious gift, and of the impassioned freedom which carried her into the presence, and to the very table, of the Pharisee. This woman was a sinner. Her history, could we read it, would, doubtless, make us weep. Whatever of wrong, or suffering, she had experienced, is concealed from us, and all we know is, that she was a sinner. It was not a case of injured innocence, palliating guilt. She was a sinner; and the compassionate Saviour himself tells us, her sins were "many."

The city mentioned in this chapter, previously to this narrative, is Nain; and nothing forbids us to adopt the supposition of some critics, that this woman lived there. She had met with Christ, then, in his public ministrations in the city of Nain. There she had heard, perhaps she was an eye-witness, of his stopping a funeral procession, and raising to life a young man, the only son of his mother, and she a widow. She had known of his feelings toward that widow; for it is said, " And when the Lord saw her, he had compassion on her, and said unto her, Weep not." This act of kindness and power had produced a great effect in the city. "And there came a fear on all; and they glorified God, saying, That a great prophet is risen up among us; and, That God hath visited his people."

In that same city, and at that time, (we have the same reason as above named to suppose,) John's two disciples had come to Jesus, to know if he were indeed the Christ. To convince them, it is said that " in that same hour, he cured many of their infirmities, and plagues, and evil spirits; and unto many that were blind he gave sight." Never had there been such scenes in that city. Wonder, joy, thanksgiving, reigned in all those streets. The impression which Christ had made on the mind of this woman was that which he intended all his miracles should produce, namely, that he had come to save men from their sins. He would not have men think that he was a mere worker of miracles; he did not put forth his power to astonish men; he used them to give effect to his exhortations, and to his promises of pardon and salvation to the guilty.

This was precisely that which this woman needed. She was an outcast, and among the offscouring of the earth. She probably felt that she had not a friend in the world. Her father's house, if that remained, she had forsaken; perhaps it was shut against her. Not a relative or former friend would speak to her. She was alone in every company; she was solitary in the throng. But what was this to the consciousness of shame; and what was the reproach of the world to a sense of unforgiven sin? Soon she must die, and be buried, with no one to weep for her; but what was this to her expected meeting with a holy God? Despair had made her his prey; no door of hope appeared, leading to restoration amongst the virtuous; she felt like a damned spirit, and waited for a deeper hell in the inevitable doom, which, she had reason to fear, would come on sinners like her.

Who can imagine her feelings when she met with Christ, and heard him preach repentance, forgiveness, and the love of God toward the vilest of the vile? Perhaps at first it only made her weep, as one in bondage awakes and weeps over a dream of his home and friends. But, when she heard of his raising the young man from the bier, out of compassion to his widowed mother; when she saw him as they brought demoniacs before him, and he cast out the devils, and the cured men threw themselves at the feet of their Saviour, she took courage; hope dawned; she began to feel that there was mercy even for her. Whether she had any interview with Christ previously to her meeting him in the Pharisee's house, we cannot tell; we only know that, in consequence of what she had heard from Christ, she found access to God. This, this, was the great truth which lifted her up from the very gates of death: that God the Saviour loves even the guilty; that sin, a whole life of sin, sins of the foulest name, sins which ruin the sinner in the view of the world, and fill his soul with the shame which leads to despair, cannot shut the sinner out from God's compassion, but that Christ had come to find such sinners, and forgive them, and make them fit for heaven.

Could there be a greater change in the feelings of the human soul than took place in her at this discovery? She began to feel that it was of use to repent. Repentance before only took the form of remorse; now, it brought her even to heaven's gate. She had begun to cherish the hope of being pardoned and saved; that God would be her Friend; that her pollution could be washed away. Let others think of her as they would, God and the Saviour would smile upon her; her peace was beginning to be like a river; and soon there was not a spirit in heaven whose joy surpassed her joy.

She was told that Christ had gone to eat with the Pharisee. She felt that she must see him. She was determined to see him; no earthly power should keep her from her Saviour. But there must be some seeming apology, or object, in her intrusion into the Pharisee's house. She remembered the customary act of hospitality when strangers came into the house. The thought was enough for her. She would mingle with the servants, would take the place of those who anointed the guest. She hastened for the ointment; she saw the beautiful, the costly alabaster box upon the shelf of the apothecary. Though it were the most costly box that he could sell, it was not too much for her love. Her heart, her soul, her all, she had given to Christ; that box she would have, even if she spent all to buy it. Then, without being invited by the Pharisee, or by his guest, she pressed into the house, and loved and worshipped Him who had brought her to repentance and to hope by his assurances of pardon to the lost. Love seeks for gifts to bestow upon the beloved object, and the Saviour excites the desire in one who has been forgiven, to bring offerings to him. Thus, in times of special interest in the subject of religion, we frequently find articles of jewelry in the contributions to religious and charitable objects, special donations are made in the form of thank offerings, which are secret expressions of love and gratitude to Christ, corresponding to the alabaster box of ointment and the 'pound of spikenard very costly.' These gifts have the effect to strengthen the confidence of the giver in his feelings toward the object of his love.

The woman in the text showed her confidence in her love to Christ by this voluntary offering.

We are taught a most interesting, practical truth by this narrative, viz.: —

THE REPRESENTATION OF CHRIST, AS A SAVIOUR, IS THE ONLY EFFECTUAL MEANS OF BRINGING TO REPENTANCE THOSE WHO ARE CONSCIOUS OF GUILT.

To preach hope and mercy, through atoning blood to those who feel their sins, is the appointed way of bringing them to God. Heaven and hope do more in preaching than hell and despair. Our object must be to persuade men when we use the terrors of the Lord; the law, with its requirements and penalty, must point to Christ; otherwise, we awaken only wrath, or sullen recklessness, or despair. Our ministry, with all its alarms and threatenings, must be a ministry of reconciliation, and the definition of our great object must be this: "But we preach Christ crucified."

Let us suppose that, instead of meeting with Christ, this woman had been addressed by one of the Jewish teachers, who should have undertaken merely to reprove, upbraid, and terrify the sinner, by an exhibition of her guilt and its consequences. He might have filled her with remorse; he might have plunged her into the depths of sorrow; and the effect would have been to fasten upon her conscience that burden of guilt which, perhaps, before was greater than she could bear. It might, indeed, have reformed her, but still she would have been likely to die under her increasing sense of unworthiness; and every day that she continued to live a better life would have only brought to her mind, in contrast, the wickedness of her former days. She might have sunk into the grave under the corroding effect of shame and sorrow; or her unavailing efforts to recover the confidence of the world might have made her desperate; and she would then have plunged again into sin. She might have said, I know that I am as guilty and vile as you represent; but my character is gone; my happiness is blasted; I am ruined for this world and the next. I cannot suffer more than I have suffered already, and I am determined to take the consequences of my sin.

We see this very effect of conviction of sin in many who sit under the preaching of the gospel. For some reasons, which it is not difficult to explain, men are apt to despair, grow reckless, and thus resist the influences of the gospel. One reason is, they have failed in their efforts to overcome their sins, and having fallen anew under the power of temptation, they conclude that there is no hope of their ever being any better; and thus they listen to preaching with no interest, or only to be hardened by it. When such men hear exhibitions of guilt, and of their exposure to punishment, it sometimes creates in them a desperate and daring state of mind. The more vivid you make their sins, and future misery, to their thoughts, either they are angry, and sullen, and hate God, and religion, and every thing connected with religion, or, they settle down in a stupid and brutish condition. 'The law worketh wrath.' It makes men think of wrath, and only wrath, and it fills them with wrath. Now, if preaching has this for its great object, or if it produces this as its chief effect, to make men feel guilty, and does nothing else, its tendency is to ruin the soul. The gospel may be professedly preached so as to destroy the effect which the gospel was intended to produce. Conviction of sin is useful only as a means of preparing the mind to receive the offers of the gospel; but if we make men feel guilty, and do nothing more, we are like a physician who deals with nothing but a probe, and never mollifies the wound, nor binds it up with ointment. It has an equally bad effect never to present any thing to the minds of men but mercy and hope. This begets stupidity and carelessness, and is like laying ointment on a wound which has not been searched and cleansed. Both extremes are ruinous. The great secret in the successful preaching of the gospel is, to make men feel that they are sinners, and that, as sinners, they are the objects of divine compassion; that their sins are as scarlet, but may be white as snow; red like crimson, but that they may be as wool.

The preaching of Christ crucified will produce conviction of sin and repentance better than any thing else; for this theme will lead us to be full in our instructions about the nature and extent of the sinner's guilt, and its fearful consequences, which demanded such a ransom. Where conscience has been enlightened from any sources, and the truth has been felt respecting our guilt and danger as sinners, it is the duty, and the blessed privilege, of ministers to hold forth the gospel of reconciliation. All who have had the care of children, or have been called to use moral influences with their fellow-men, know that law and its sanctions are instruments inferior to love and mercy; that it is easier to melt than to break, to draw than to drive, and that persuasion triumphs where conviction and admonition have utterly failed. God regards this principle in his creatures, a principle established by his own creative wisdom; and, accordingly, the gospel, rather than the law, is the perfection of his progressive administration in a world of sin and a world of hope. 'For what the law could not do, in that it was weak through the' obstinate and despairing tendencies of sinful 'flesh, God sending his own Son in the likeness of sinful flesh, and for sin,' has been able to accomplish.

In dealing with sinners, and in dealing with our selves as sinners, we never ought to forget, that to break the law of God, times without number, is not so great guilt as to reject mercy. Therefore, when we are conscious of guilt, we ought not to feel that we have shut ourselves out from hope. This is not all. Though we have oftentimes rejected mercy, and turned away from Christ, we ought not to feel that even this is an unpardonable sin. None of us understand fully, even if we think we have learned much of it, none of us fully understand the love and compassion of God toward the guilty. To blaspheme the Holy Ghost, to speak profanely of his gracious influences, seals a sinner's doom. Any thing short of this, though it were blasphemy against Christ, is pardonable; and no one may feel that there is no hope for him, whatever his sins may have been, if he has not spoken against the Spirit. It is wrong for the unconverted to indulge in despondency and gloom about themselves. Their argument against themselves is, that they have sinned against light and conviction; that they have known their duty, and have refused to do it; and that they have offended God beyond the probability of mercy. They shut the door of hope upon themselves; but God opens it continually, and assures them that his mercy is above the heavens.

There is one illustration of the way in which God

treats us, as sinners, which will serve to open to our minds his feelings toward the guilty. I refer to the way in which we are warned and cautioned against the lusts of the flesh. Such warnings and cautions are so often accompanied by expressions of love and tenderness as to make you think that the connection is not accidental. Hear how the Holy Ghost speaks to us, in warning us of certain sins, the consciousness of which disposes us, perhaps, more than any thing else, to indulge fear and despair. "Dearly beloved," he says, (mark the kindness of the appeal,) "Dearly beloved, I beseech you, as strangers and pilgrims, abstain from fleshly lusts, which war against the soul." Again: "Having these promises, dearly beloved, let us cleanse ourselves from all filthiness of the flesh and spirit." Again: "Be ye, therefore, followers of God, as dear children; and walk in love, as Christ also hath loved us." Then follows an exhortation against uncleanness. Once more: "When Christ, who is your life, shall appear, then shall ye also appear with him in glory." What follows? "Mortify, therefore, your members which are upon the earth." O, what tenderness there is in God, in dealing with us as sinners, in this world of mercy. "For he knoweth our frame, he remembereth that we are dust."

This example of it, now quoted, illustrates the whole tenor of the divine feelings toward us, in seeking to withdraw us from sin, and raise us to glory and virtue.

Now, upon this same principle of encouraging the guilty to return, of awakening hope and effort in the minds of sinners, by a sense of his compassion toward the lost, God sent his Son to be the Saviour of the world. Christ began his work by acts of kindness toward the poorest, the lowest, the most helpless; and toward the greatest sinners. The objects which surrounded him, day after day, as subjects of his grace, and in which his soul delighted, were such as now fill our almshouses, insane hospitals, infirmaries, and our chambers of protracted sickness and disease, together with the subjects of demoniacal possession. But he had an object in the bestowment of his healing power upon these sufferers, beyond their relief from pain. He said to those whom he healed, when he saw that they were prepared for his word of grace, "Thy sins are forgiven thee." Matthew, and Zaccheus, and other publicans and sinners, found in him a Friend to the soul, and experienced in his mercy a joy surpassing that of mitigated pain. By his acts of kindness to the lost and wretched, he established, in the minds of the common people, this truth, that there is love in the heart of God for every miserable sinner; that his vileness, and his abandonment by the world, only commend him to God as an object of his compassion; that the Son of God came down from the skies to save the worst of men; and that it is impossible for a sinner to be sunk too low for his hand to find him, or for his grace to lift him up. Christ could not look on human woe without compassion. He could not see the widow following her only son to the grave, without pity, and he spoiled the monster, death, of his prey. John the Baptist, in prison, wished to know whether Christ was indeed that Messiah promised in the garden of Eden, foretold by prophets, and sung by the inspired bards; whom kings waited for, and the wise men went to worship. How did he convince John that he was that Messiah? He called a motley crowd of blind, lame, leprous, withered, squalid sufferers around him, with here and there a raving demoniac, and healed them. Then, to the two disciples that came to look at his credentials from heaven, and the sign manual from God, and to know if he were the Christ, he said, 'Go and show John again those things which ye do hear and see.' These are my credentials; this crowd is my witness that I am he.

As the Saviour of the soul, he used these proofs of his love and power to draw the guilty and perishing sinner to his side. Such a sinner was she whose brief history we read in our text. Did Christ upbraid her, and send her away convinced of sin and of judgment to come? What wonderful charm did he employ to work such an overwhelming conviction in her, and, at the same time, make this conviction the means of the greatest joy she had ever felt? It was love and mercy that saved her; it was forgiveness that broke her hard heart; it was confidence in God and Christ that made her, a weak and friendless woman, courageous and strong. The Pharisees and scribes might have convinced her of her guilt, but she would never have bought an alabaster box of ointment to anoint their feet. "Behold the Lamb of God, that taketh away the sin of the world;"—it was this direction, imparted by the divine Spirit, that rescued her from despair. In the dark recesses of her guilt, hope and peace were shed abroad by one who had words of comfort for her, and wounded her only that he might bind her up. It could be said of her soul, as it is said of heaven, The Lamb is the light thereof.

Many are the instances in which conversion seems to be the immediate consequence of love and gratitude, and no anguish is felt, at the time, in view of sin. A need of Christ, as a Saviour, of course exists; but the overwhelming emotion is approbation of God's character and dealings, complacency in some particular attribute, gratitude to Christ for what he has done, an assurance of safety in looking at the cross of Christ, a conviction of the infinite willingness of God to save sinners. There is nothing more absurd than to suppose that there is one process through which every mind must go, in ob taining peace with God. Some have fallen asleep upon their pillows with strong crying and tears, and have waked from sleep in the morning, feeling that all creation was praising God, and with a heart to praise him too. Submission to God, in Christ, had taken place in that weeping, and, as a consequence, joy came in the morning, with the return of consciousness, after the composure of sleep. We cannot say that this, or that, or another order of thought and feeling is the way to find peace with God.

Are you, then, a sinner? are you discouraged? are you almost, if not quite, inclined to abandon hope, and all effort to save your soul, and to let the consequences of guilt come as fast and as fearful as they may? Does conversion, does religion, seem to you a mighty work, unattainable by you? and do you sink down, dismayed, at what you must do to be a Christian, and in despair at the recollection of past efforts, so fruitless, and, as you think, aggravating your guilt? How was it with this woman in our text? Love and gratitude led her on, and a sense of guilt and ruin made her come to the Saviour. Begin to love Christ, and all the conviction, and repentance, and faith, and hope, that you ever wished for, will flow forth from a regenerated heart; for 'he that loveth is born of God, and knoweth God.' I would go, then, to my secret place, as this woman went to the Pharisee's house, to find Christ. Press your way to him, as she did with her box of ointment in her hand, to that chamber where Christ waits for you; there begin to thank and praise him for all that he suffered and has done for you. Think of nothing else; your sins, your ill desert, your past ill success, your future weakness, your fears; let all be forgotten, and begin to love your infinite Redeemer and Friend. What a way to be saved is this: to love the Saviour of the world. Thousands have proved it sure; why may not you?

"Canst thou not love the Friend who died
  Thy burden to assume?
Who shrunk not from the crown of thorns,
  The scourge, the cross, the tomb?

"If heavy is thy weight of guilt,
  Thy love should greater be;
Then He, whose blood for man was spilt,
  Will shed his peace on thee."

SERMON VIII.

MARTHA AND MARY.

LUKE X. 38, 39.

NOW IT CAME TO PASS, AS THEY WENT, THAT HE ENTERED INTO A CERTAIN VILLAGE; AND A CERTAIN WOMAN, NAMED MARTHA, RECEIVED HIM INTO HER HOUSE. AND SHE HAD A SISTER CALLED MARY, WHICH ALSO SAT AT JESUS' FEET, AND HEARD HIS WORD.

THE characters of these two friends of Christ have always been deeply interesting to the readers of the New Testament. They are mentioned together in three places by the evangelists. The first is in the chapter of which the text is a part.

Martha seems to have been the head of the family, composed of herself, her sister Mary, and her brother Lazarus. That they were in easy, if not affluent, circumstances, appears from several incidents in their history. On the occasion mentioned in the text, it seems that Christ, and probably some, if not all, of his disciples with him, who went with him in his daily walks, were entertained by Martha at her house. The sudden entrance of so many strangers imposed much care and responsibility upon the head of the household; and hospitality being a great study, and one of the most important of customs in the East, the mistress of the family had many things to think of and to do, especially for such a guest as she esteemed Christ to be. We may infer that Martha was a woman who took great pains with every thing which she did, and made much of every duty, and perhaps of every trouble; being of an anxious disposition, and yet a woman of great energy, of stirring habits, thorough, and ambitious to have every thing done in the best manner. So, as soon as her guests had entered the house, it may be without much previous notice, her whole soul was absorbed with entertaining them. The servants must provide water for the hands and feet of the guests; refreshments must be immediately set before them, and afterward a repast in the form of a regular meal.

But Martha was not content to let things proceed in a simple manner, with a word now and then to direct the course of affairs; but she laid herself out to do more than was necessary, and was 'cumbered about much serving.' In the midst of her anxiety to provide and arrange her entertainment, she missed her sister, and found that she was seated, according to the custom of inquirers in those days, at the feet of Christ, and was listening eagerly to his conversation.

The excitement and hurry of an important occasion are not favorable to a calm and equable temper, nor to deliberate and well-considered words; and Martha at this time, in an impatient and fretful mood, quite forgot the proprieties of life, and the kindness due to a sister, by appealing to her guest against that sister. Entering the room where Jesus and the company were sitting, with Mary at his feet, she said, "Lord, dost thou not care that my sister hath left me to serve alone? Bid her, therefore, that she help me." Her wish was, that the guests should excuse them both until all needful preparations were made for the repast; her only care at Jesus' presence in her house being, What shall we provide for him to eat?

Not so with Mary. It was an inestimable blessing, in her view, to have the Saviour under her roof. She saw that he was neither famished nor weary; and so, instead of occupying herself with the thought of an entertainment, she took that opportunity to satisfy the wants of her soul, which hungered and thirsted after righteousness. Now she had found one who could resolve all her difficulties in religion, lead her to an established hope, satisfy her desire to know more of God and spiritual things, and comfort her with the consolations of religion. Suppose that her brother Lazarus were then travelling in Persia or India, and Christ were a friend who had just arrived from those parts, and had come to her house to tell her that he had seen Lazarus. It would have been out of place for her to leave him before obtaining from him all the information which she so much desired, and leave him, too, to provide a feast, as though all that he came for was to eat. Now, Christ had come into her dwelling to tell her of things transcendently interesting and important, in which her soul was wrapped up; and could she, should she, leave him, and think only of a handsome entertainment at table? That would be disparaging to her guest; it would embarrass him to see that his coming had been the signal for such dismay and labor; it would be treating him as no visitor loves to be treated who comes for an important errand, or from love for his friends, and is not intent merely on being warmed and fed. At a proper time, no doubt, Mary would do her part toward providing a suitable entertainment; there would be a season in the visit when she might properly be excused, and when a due regard for him, whom she had engaged so long in conversation, might require her to leave him for a while. But Martha, from the time that he came into the house, was cumbered with her plans and labors to serve him as a guest; was taking no pleasure, and receiving no profit from him in the great concerns of her soul; and as the sorrow of the world worketh death, so worldly cares had a deadly influence on her feelings, and she wished that Christ, who knew what was due to strangers, and how much needed to be done to prepare an entertainment, would send her sister to her household work.

"And Jesus answered, and said unto her, Martha, Martha, thou art careful and troubled about many things."

Here we must understand Christ as referring to her general character and disposition. The idea, suggested even by some good men, that Christ meant to say that Martha was unduly anxious to provide many things for their entertainment, and that only one article of food was really needful, is, in the language of another good man and able critic, almost "unpardonable." The Saviour's concluding remark about Mary shows that he refers to the general disposition and choice. He says to Martha, twice repeating her name, for emphasis, 'Thou art careful and troubled about many things.' Every thing excites in you an anxious, troubled mind. You magnify every thing which you have to do, by disproportioned solicitude; and by being wholly absorbed in domestic cares and labors, are really losing sight of that one great thing, which alone is of real importance. The Saviour then approved of Mary's disposition, as of one who had placed things in their true light, and had chosen the good part which should never be taken away from her.

The characters of these friends of Christ, thus far,

suggest two thoughts, which we will consider, before we turn a leaf in their history.

1. *There may be sin in being very busy.*

It is not enough for us, it will not satisfy Christ, nor be for our justification in the great day, that we were constantly at work. The question will be, What were you doing? Always working with your hands and head, and finding no time to sit at Christ's feet; opening the store, or shop, or room, early; leaving it only for a hasty meal; closing it, tired and sleepy, at night; and later and more fatigued on Saturday night than any other; sitting at your desk or table incessantly, with no time for God and heaven; or working from morning to night for the family, to provide the meat that perisheth, or raiment, and other necessaries of life? God requires diligence, and rebukes those who deal with a slack hand. But to how many would the Saviour's just reproof apply: 'Thou art careful and troubled about many things;' to many who think that they are the best of fathers and mothers, and sons and daughters, and tradesmen and mechanics. They who think only of this life and their business, of the body and the supply of its wants, with no reference to the soul and eternity, are like a ship's company who should put to sea with nothing but provisions on board. On they sail, from day to day; but they only know that they are going across the water; they have no freight for trade, nor money to buy a cargo; and yet they work hard at the ropes, buffet the storms, escape shipwreck, endure cold and heat, only with the thought of living from day to day. Such is a picture of many who are sailing over this sea of time, and are doing nothing but getting across the sea. What will become of them there, or what they shall do, they seldom, if ever, think.

Christ says, Take heed that your hearts be not overcharged with surfeiting, and drunkenness, and cares of this life. What company is this in which many will find their employment, which they think so exemplary? — the cares of life are classed with surfeiting and drunkenness. Yes, there may be sin in being busy. Are you seeking first the kingdom of God and his righteousness? Do you work merely to live, or do you live for man's chief end, to glorify God and enjoy him forever? If not, the Saviour reproves you; though you were doing all this for his bodily comfort, he reproves you; and surely, then, if it be for yourselves and families, he reproves you; and sets in contrast before you the example of one who has a higher aim, a nobler spirit, an enduring portion.

Some say, I cannot attend to the subject of religion, my business is so great and pressing. But who made it so? Has God thus disabled you? Have you not yourself made the net which confines you?

and do you not feel satisfied with it? God will not accept it as an excuse for neglecting him.

2. *Religion is the only thing which we cannot lose.* What will be the result of all these careful and troubled thoughts, and the end of these busy days and nights, and of this occupation, which is so incessant that you cannot save your soul? What will you have to show for them in a dying hour, at the bar of God, and in the other world? Every thing is worthless which is not subservient to religion and the soul. 'Whose shall these things be which thou hast provided?' and where shall they be for whom thou hast provided them? It is a most interesting sight — Mary sitting at Christ's feet, absorbed, for the time, in the one thing needful, and securing for herself that good part which change and death cannot take from her. Every one ought sincerely to ask himself, at his daily business, — he should put the question frequently; let him write it, if he will, inside his desk, or in something which comes in occasional use, — What am I living for? Let him consider whether, by all his care and trouble, he is securing any thing which will avail him for more than a little period of time, which, compared with eternity, is like a drop of water on the finger's end, taken from the measureless sea. O, sad choice, to prefer the world, and care, and labor, and the

pleasure of being indifferent about religion, and freedom from anxiety about the soul, to the blessedness of being a child of God. All that indifference will be taken away from you, with every thing else, and you must be intensely interested in the things unseen and eternal. Look at those busy hands. Soon, folded over your breast, in your long, long sleep, they will consume away in the grave.

> "And must this body die,
> This mortal frame decay?
> And must these active limbs of mine
> Lie mouldering in the clay?"

Where shall the soul that never dies, find herself then? What has she, what am I providing for her, which shall never be taken away from her?

Thus far we see these two sisters representing two great classes, the one, losing sight of the one thing needful, by inordinate occupation with the duties and cares of life, and the other, seeking first the kingdom of God and his righteousness. The sisters of the same family, the brothers, the husband and wife, and all of them together, are admonished by this family picture to consider how Christ regards the manner of their life. 'One thing is needful.' What place and proportion does this one thing needful hold in our thoughts?

We cannot conclude with certainty that Martha was not, up to this time, a pious woman; and yet we fail to get satisfying evidence of it. Some think that, because it is said of Mary, she 'also' sat at Jesus' feet, it is implied that Martha, too, was of the same religious disposition with her sister. But the sitting at Jesus' feet, here spoken of, does not refer to a habit or disposition, but to a certain act done at that time; and the word, 'also,' rather joins Mary with the twelve disciples than Martha with Mary. The comparison which Christ makes in favor of Mary is a strong reflection upon Martha. Still, we read, "Now Jesus loved Martha, and Mary, and her brother Lazarus." Whether this was more than the love which he felt for the young ruler, who, nevertheless, like Martha, was also cumbered with the world, so that he went away from Christ sorrowful, we cannot tell. But we will pass to another chapter in her history, and there we shall see evidence that Martha had then, if not before, like Mary, chosen the good part.

Affliction visited the house where Jesus had been a guest. The brother was sick. The sisters sent a pathetic message to Christ, saying, 'Lord, he whom thou lovest is sick.' The prayer reached him, and touched his heart; and we see in his conduct the manner in which he frequently hears and treats our prayers. 'When, therefore, he heard that he was sick, he abode two days still in the same place where he was;' and in the mean time, Lazarus died. The all-seeing eye of Christ had been upon him, and saw him die; for he said to his disciples, 'Lazarus is dead. And I am glad, for your sakes, that I was not there, to the intent ye may believe. Nevertheless, let us go unto him.'

The sisters heard that he was coming; and here we have them before us again, each in her proper character, affected, however, by new circumstances, and, in Martha's case, by some great change for the better. Observe how the natural disposition of the two sisters runs into their religious character and conduct. "Then Martha, as soon as she knew that he was coming, went and met him; but Mary sat still in the house." This contemplative sister, inclined to deep, serious views and feelings, in her affliction had no disposition to move abroad, even to meet Christ. Surely now her sister appears to the best advantage. Mary broods over her affliction, nurses her sorrows, indulges in the luxury of grief. The news that Jesus is coming stirs Martha to go and meet him; and she goes to him with as heavy a burden of sorrow as Mary felt; but how much wiser than she, to go and lay it at Jesus' feet. 'There are last that shall be first.' Would we not have supposed that Mary would have been the first to go to Christ?

The prompt, active, energetic spirit of Martha goes with her into religion; the Saviour's rebuke had been blessed to her; she will show that she is no longer careful and troubled about worldly things; she, also, will sit at Jesus' feet, and hear his words.

Martha's conversation with Christ shows her to have had faith; still it was weak; and yet, no weaker than that of Mary, who, afterward, said the same words: "Lord, if thou hadst been here, my brother had not died." Martha professed to believe that whatsoever he should ask of God, God would give it to him. She forgot, or did not understand, that, 'as the Father raiseth up the dead, and quickeneth them, even so the Son quickeneth whom he will;' 'And as the Father hath life in himself, even so hath he given to the Son to have life in himself.' Martha's words, "Even now I know that whatsoever thou wilt ask of God, God will give it thee," seem to imply that she was thinking of her brother being raised from the dead, and yet she does not give form to that thought; it seems somewhat like one of those presentiments which are unaccountable. Even when Christ said, 'Thy brother shall rise again,' she did not apply the words to an immediate resurrection, but to the last great day. Her remark respecting it shows, that the hope of that far-distant resurrection failed to satisfy her, as it fails to satisfy us when we feel the strong desire to bring back the lost one to our present enjoyment and love. Christ, on this occasion, uttered words which, it is generally agreed, are not equalled in sublimity, except where it is written, "And God said, Let there be light, and there was light." "Jesus said unto her, I am the resurrection and the life." Every paraphrase and explanation fails to make these words more impressive. "I am the resurrection." What is that resurrection? What will it be for all the pious dead to rise? Christ is the author of it, and the author of all that follows it —eternal life. We are willing to worship Christ as God, at such words as these. He adds words which turn the thoughts of the world to him, as the Author of salvation: "He that believeth in me, though he were dead, yet shall he live;" and wonderful still, "and whosoever liveth, and believeth in me, shall never die"; death shall not be to him what nature makes it, and sinners find it; but it will be to him an experience of Christ's presence and love, the waking to life, by the soul, instead of its falling asleep. 'Believest thou this?' said Christ to his weeping friend. She professed her faith there. 'Yea, Lord, I believe that thou art the Christ, the Son of God, which should come into the world.' Martha is surely a believer, and we may no more look to see her careful and troubled about many things.

Once she called Mary away from Christ, and prayed Christ to reprove her sister, at his feet; now, she goes in haste, and sends her sister to those same feet. "And when she had so said, she went away, and called Mary, her sister, secretly," (because the Jews sought to stone Christ,) "saying, The Master is come, and calleth for thee." Affliction, joined with the Saviour's reproof, had been blessed to Martha. "The rod and reproof give wisdom"; and "a reproof entereth more into a wise man, than a hundred stripes into a fool."

Mary, in her turn, now comes again before us. Does she remain at home, sullen and unbelieving, or harboring sorrow at Christ's omission to come and save the precious life of her brother? 'As soon as she heard that, she arose quickly, and came unto him. And when she was come where Jesus was, and saw him, she fell down at his feet, saying unto him, Lord, if thou hadst been here, my brother had not died.' More passionate than Martha, her nature disposed more to love and tenderness, she falls at those feet again, where she had chosen and received eternal happiness.

We must pass by the events at the grave; nor will we stop to contemplate that scene where these sisters received that brother to life again. Their love and transport at the sight of each other, and of their Saviour, presented the most perfect representation of the great rising day which is on record. That day may be, to you, all and more than this resurrection and meeting were to these sisters and their brother. See in them a picture of your family circle at the grave, on the morning of the resurrection. May it be a picture of our households. Can we say of our families, as John Eliot said of his, "We are all in Christ, or with Christ"? If we can, the opened grave at Bethany, with the scene around it, is an emblem of our burying-place, at the last day. If not, it is because all have not chosen the good part which shall never be taken from them.

Several topics are suggested by this second chapter in the history of these friends of Christ, upon which, however, a remark in passing will suffice.

1. Judicious and kind treatment has great power. It probably saved Martha's soul. We should be willing to give such reproof. We should be willing to receive it, so that our souls may live.

2. When a friend is sick, it is a great comfort if we can say of him to Christ, 'Lord, he whom thou lovest is sick.' If physicians heal him, Christ does it by them. If he dies, it will be for the glory of God, the last earthly act, to him, of redeeming love.

3. When our friends die, we should not sit still, to nourish grief, but go to Christ with it. "Trust in him at all times; ye people, pour out your hearts before him; God is a refuge for us."

We come now to the third and last scene in

which these friends of Christ appear to us. Jesus is within a week of his crucifixion. 'Then Jesus, six days before the Passover, came to Bethany, where Lazarus was which had been dead, whom he raised from the dead. There,' (Mark says that it was at the house of Simon the leper — probably a friend of Martha and Mary —) 'they made him a supper; and Martha served.' Yes, Martha, of course we shall find you serving. Your energy, zeal, and hospitality are not quenched by your religion. You are a noble-hearted woman; we will put tenderness into our love for Mary, and respect into our love for you. We love you all the more for your original fault, now corrected; we love you the more for having once blamed you. Mary, so far as we see her, never went astray; but now, we almost rejoice more over you than over ninety and nine like her. We have a fellow feeling for you, because we are so much like you, careful and troubled about many things, and tempted to impatience and haste; and it seems as though you, like Christ, could be touched with the feeling of our infirmities. We love you for taking reproof so well, loving the hand that smote you; we love you for being willing still to serve, with no wounded pride, nor rankling thought at having been corrected. If Mary was more like an angel, you are more like a redeemed sinner; and those redeemed sinners who have had the most to contend with, will owe more to divine grace, and sing the sweetest praise.

"But Lazarus was one of them that sat at table with him."

There breathed the man, one of the very few whom death has released, for a season, from his awful grasp, for whom the grave had opened her doors that he might escape. He sits there with his Redeemer. We, at the table of Christ, in the presence of our Redeemer, have been raised from a death more terrible than the king of terrors, and, indeed, from that which alone makes death the king of terrors. Let the feelings of Lazarus on that occasion be our feelings, his gratitude and love ours, his faith and confidence ours. It is an emblem, too, of a risen church at the table of Christ. We shall sit at that table of Christ, in heaven, with all his friends, where the thought that we must die will no more come to us, as no doubt it did to Lazarus, at that table; but we shall sit with him who is the resurrection and the life, and our supper shall be no more the showing forth of his death, but the marriage supper of the Lamb.

The scene, and the history of these friends of Christ, now closes with an incident as interesting as any previous part of it.

"Then took Mary a pound of ointment of spikenard, very costly, and anointed the feet of Jesus, and wiped his feet with her hair; and the house was filled with the odor of the ointment."

This is one of the incidents which show that this family were in circumstances of more than comfort. That ointment was not a Syrian product, but an imported article, the celebrated Indian spikenard, a compound of the most rare and costly aromatics, of which spikenard was the basis, and which gave the compound its name. It is mentioned in Solomon's Song with the chief of perfumes. The poet Horace speaks of a small stone box of it as worth a cask of wine. Judas Iscariot said that it might have been sold for three hundred pence; each of those pence, or denarii, being about seventeen cents of our money, making the ointment worth about fifty dollars. Very precious, indeed, was such an anointing, and Judas remonstrated at what he pretended to consider an enormous waste. The Saviour justified Mary. Her love seeks for the most costly offering; and let her bring it. She seems to have had some information of Christ's approaching death; for Christ had told the twelve apostles of it, and from his regard for that family at Bethany, we may suppose that he had told them. That anointing, then, was an honor done to him in view of his approaching end; and Mary's love to her Saviour, and the character of that Saviour as God's Anointed, warranted this costly offering. Mark says, "She poured it on his head." John does not contradict this, but he adds the more striking incident that his feet also were anointed.

This ointment was nearly liquid, of exceeding delicacy, used by rich women for the hair; to which Mary appropriately applied the superfluous ointment from the Saviour's feet. The house was filled with the odorous balsam; and the more extensive fragrance of the deed fulfils the word of Christ as recorded by Mark: "Wheresoever this gospel shall be preached throughout the whole world, this also that she hath done shall be spoken of for a memorial of her."

We have now seen Mary three times, and every time at the Saviour's feet; first, as a learner; secondly, as a mourner; thirdly, as a servant and worshipper. She is there to-day. She has long since cast her crown at those feet. She enjoys to-day that good part which cannot be taken away from her. Lazarus is dead. Neither he, nor any other mere mortal, was "the first fruits of them that slept." Death again brought him to the narrow house, but it must have been a joyful day for him when he returned to heaven, like an angel revisiting his throne. Martha has exchanged her toils and cares for the rest of heaven; but her active mind, and heart, and hands

> "find sweet employ
> In that eternal world of joy."

Ye friends of Christ, we must copy your example, catch your spirit, love and serve your Saviour, and reign with him and with you. As they would celebrate the sacramental supper, as they would go away from it, as they would live hereafter, in view of such a privilege, Lord, help us so to eat of this bread, and drink of this cup.

Several reflections are suggested by this whole narrative.

1. *The Saviour is a friend of individuals and of families.* That house in Bethany was a place where he loved to resort. The three inmates deeply interested him; and with regard to two of them, we have seen some of the obvious reasons.

He loved John, also. He would have loved that young ruler, had not that amiable youth been like many others, foolish, and gone away sorrowful from his presence. Christ has objects of special affection; they are such as love him and serve him with no ordinary love, and whose characters are such as he, the perfect Judge of character, can approve. Blessed be his name, they are none of them perfect. But he loves to help them in their endeavors to be so. He loves certain families; families of prayer; families whose members love one another; families where he is exalted, and his cause and his friends are cherished, and his name is most precious, and where the whole life of the household is one hymn of praise to Christ, a fragrant sacrifice of devoted service to his honor and glory.

2. *Christ loves special acts and testimonials of love.* If you have children, and earnestly pray the Saviour to use them for his glory, he will be pleased with the offering and consecration.

If you ever have a gift which you desire to make to him, some gold, or silver, or ornament, which no one requires you to give away, and with love to Christ you come to him in prayer, and break that box upon his head and his feet, he will love you for it, and you will love him. But it must not be a mere sense of duty that prompts it.

If you have only 'two mites, which make a farthing,' and they are your all, and yet your love and gratitude impel you to offer them to Christ, and any one would remonstrate, Christ takes your part, and says, Let them alone. He will take the gift, and enrich your souls. Ministers sometimes hear of incidents among their people, in their contributions, for example, to foreign missions—which make them feel that perhaps Christ loves individuals among them very much. Some of you shed spikenard on the Saviour, bestowing your gifts upon him through his cause, or his suffering friends; and wherever you go, you will be sure to carry the joy of it in your heart, as Mary carried in her hair the perfume which she took from Jesus' feet. It was little, it may be, in your esteem, and you thought only how small it seemed; but you were not ashamed of it, nor was Christ. Let us make every contribution to the cause of Christ an express offering to him; sometimes let us bring special gifts to him who gave his blood for us. The oftener, like Mary, we are at his feet, for any purpose, to learn, to be comforted, or to give gifts, the wiser, the safer, the happier, shall we be. A lady once had a rare and beautiful plant, which bloomed with such surpassing richness that it seemed due to her sovereign, and, as the highest expression of her love and respect, she sent it to the Queen. With the same feelings did Hannah give her Samuel, the object of such desire and love, to God; and, more distinguished still, a poor widow, no doubt with the same emotions, in offering one farthing to her God, 'cast in more than they all.' Let secret prayer and consecration precede religious and charitable offerings, and they will be new cords of love between your soul and Christ.

3. *Whenever we come to the table of Christ, we may say, by faith, This is Bethany.* Can there be places or scenes on earth more interesting to Christ than those in which his people partake of the memorials of his death? If he is ever specially present with us, it is in connection with that which he bids us do in remembrance of him, and which, more than any thing else, reminds him of us.

Would that we could always receive him and commune with him in the spirit of Mary, who forgot every thing but Christ as soon as he entered her dwelling.

Would that we could honor him by a room full of guests. We have invited several hundreds of our friends to join with us in communion with Christ at his table, but hitherto they have said, I pray thee have me excused.

But, after all, our chief thought at the table of Christ must be with regard to ourselves, if we would profit by the sacramental season. 'The Master is come, and calleth for thee.' Let him search your heart, reprove you, not sparing your faults, but setting them in order before you. If he would treat us all as he did Martha, it would be well for us. He knows our faults; we may also say to him, with David, "Thou knowest my foolishness." Let us never go away without feeling reproved for some particular fault or sin. Nor may he depart without bearing with him some new proofs of our love, some purposes of amendment, a consecration to him of all that we have and are, and with new bonds between him and us, whose influence shall be felt by us not only in life and in death, but when we shall 'EAT AND DRINK AT HIS TABLE, IN HIS KINGDOM.'

SERMON IX.

SIMON THE CYRENIAN.

LUKE XXIII. 26.

AND AS THEY LED HIM AWAY, THEY LAID HOLD UPON ONE SIMON, A CYRENIAN, COMING OUT OF THE COUNTRY, AND ON HIM THEY LAID THE CROSS, THAT HE MIGHT BEAR IT AFTER JESUS.

THE cross was so ignominious and hateful, that no menial servant was willing to carry it to the place of execution, and the people were unwilling that any man who was not in disgrace should be compelled to bear it through the public ways.

It would seem that when they led Jesus away to be crucified, they laid the transverse beam of the cross upon him, according to the custom of making the criminal bear the instrument of his own torture and death. But either out of compassion to Christ, which is hardly probable, or because his strength, reduced by previous sufferings, was insufficient for the load, or because they feared that their victim, who was already much exhausted by the loss of blood, might faint and die before they had executed their purposes, they found it expedient to relieve him of the burden. John says, "And they took Jesus, and led him away. And he, bearing his cross, went forth into a place called the place of a skull." But the other evangelists say that another bore the cross. Both statements are consistent. Christ carried his cross through the city, and was then relieved of it, as one of the evangelists says, "when they came out."

It is generally supposed, that this Simon was suspected, or known to be a friend, or a disciple, of Christ. Commentators agree in this impression. The reason seems to be, that only one who was odious ever had such ignominy put upon him as to bear a cross in public. Mark says, that 'this man was the father of Alexander and Rufus,' who are thus named familiarly, as though they were two disciples of Christ, well known. Two of the three evangelists who mention him, however, use the word 'compel,' in speaking of the act of the people in laying the cross upon him. Still, this may be intended merely to describe the act as it would appear generally to spectators, without intending to intimate the feelings of Simon at the force which the people would naturally use, whether he were, or were not, a friend.

He was on his way from the country into the city, when the crowd met him as they went to the execution. For some reason, he was a marked man; perhaps of such ill repute that the people felt at liberty to lay hold on him, and compel him to perform this most degrading and revolting service of carrying a cross to the place of punishment. It may have been that he was a fugitive from justice; or that he had made himself notorious by former crimes and punishment; or that, in appearance, he was a vagrant, whom the excited populace felt it safe to insult with this compulsion.

On the other hand, it may have been the case that he had made himself offensive by some prominent act of friendship to Christ, in opposition to the popular feeling. We only know that they met him accidentally, and forced upon him a service which they thought too great a disgrace for any of their number, or for one not already ignominious; and which, perhaps, no one of the disciples of Christ would have undertaken to perform, without, at first, a feeling of abhorrence.

While we adopt the general impression, that Simon was a friend of Christ, the possibility of doubt respecting his character and disposition affords an opportunity to speak of the different feelings which the professed followers of Christ, and men in general, have, with regard to the cross of Christ; by which I mean the different ways in which our feelings lead us to regard our religious duties. Some are like Simon, if he were an unconverted man, when compelled to bear the cross.

Suppose, then, that he was not a good man; or, at least, suppose that he was indifferent to Christ, and had taken no part, for him or against him, and was too much engrossed in his own affairs to be interested in the controversy respecting Jesus.

He was coming out of the country, and was going into the city, and, accidentally, passed along the way to Calvary at the time that the crowd were moving to the place of execution. They laid hold on him, and thrust the cross upon his shoulder. We see the angry, furious fellow, with the heavy cross laid on his unwilling neck. With oaths and curses he staggers along, restrained only by fear of the mob from resistance and flight. He deplores his bad luck that led him that way just at that moment. Had he been a few minutes earlier or later, he might have escaped this great disgrace. Now he feels that he has had a reproach put upon him which he can never wipe off. His family, his friends, or his acquaintances, will hear of this. What would they say if they could see him marching, at the head of a mob that follows the executioners, with a cross on his shoulders, helping a miserable victim on his way to Golgotha? Such a load he never bore; a heavier weight of sorrow he never expects to bear in this world. What right had the people to stop him in his lawful business?

Perhaps he had engagements in the city; perhaps he is losing some employment by this interruption. It may be that the mob will take it upon themselves to crucify him with Christ. Altogether, no man could be placed in a condition more vexatious and afflictive than his, short of death itself. He probably looked on himself as the most insulted, disgraced, and injured man on earth. His feelings toward the victim that walked before him could not have been of an agreeable nature. It may be that he vented his spite and anger upon him; it would have been natural, in his state of mind, to have had feelings of contempt and cruelty toward the sufferer, who had been the innocent occasion of his disgrace. If you wish for a picture of a man subjected against his will to do a direful act of necessity, from which he cannot escape, we have it in him who, with such feelings, bore the cross after Jesus.

But this man, with these supposed feelings, represents many who would not suspect that they could be compared to him. Yet the resemblance is striking, and far from being uncommon.

Here is a heartless professor of religion. He wishes that he had never taken upon himself the vows of God and joined the church of Christ, for he feels no interest in religion. He does not love prayer, nor the word of God, nor spiritual truths, nor spiritual pleasures. It is a trial to him to have the Lord's supper recur. He doubts whether he ought to go to the Lord's table, feeling so indifferent to Christ, and to religious duties and pleasures. He questions with himself whether he ought not to ask for a dismission from the church; but then he remembers that a church cannot dismiss him back to the world; that they have no right to give him up his vows to God; that they were only witnesses of those vows, putting them on record for him; but from his promises to God they cannot absolve him.

Perhaps, however, he could be contented to live in this secret state of apostasy, with a name to live while he is dead, saying nothing respecting his feelings, and passing on with the crowd, under a fair exterior; but there is one objection and difficulty. He wishes to do some things which are inconsistent with a Christian profession. He wishes to indulge in worldly pleasures, gratify his sinful appetites, commit gross sins to a degree which would subject him to censure from a Christian church; and from the commission and indulgence of these things he is hindered only by his fear of reproach and disgrace. Perhaps he wishes to send his children to places of amusement which are not approved by Christians generally, or to indulge in these pleasures himself. The fascinations of such pleasures are exceedingly sweet to him, and he wishes that the customs of the churches were such as to allow of such indulgences.

As it is, he leads a hard life in many things; he wishes that he could escape from his Christian profession; but alas! he has been taken in an evil hour, and compelled to bear the cross after Jesus. He looks on the world around him, and envies them their liberty; perhaps they say things to him which are peculiarly obnoxious, and their taunts against religion and godly people excite the most painful feelings in his breast — not of jealousy for the injured cause of religion and for the church of Christ, but to think that he has had the cross put on him, and that he cannot shake it off. He is not bearing that cross to heaven, but, as it were, to a place of execution; he is not a follower of Christ, in a true sense, though he walks behind him, but a victim, who is made to walk in the train of Christ. If there be an unhappy man, it is he who is compelled to govern his sinful inclinations and wishes against his will, merely from fear of public opinion; to act a forced part; to keep up the name and profession of godliness, when his heart is not in it. Such a man envies those who are out of the church; as Simon, probably, would have been willing to change places with the poorest and lowest of the wretches who were exulting about him in their freedom from that accursed cross, which he was compelled to bear. What a way to hell is the way of a false and heartless professor of religion. It would seem that the god of this world must have some special malice against certain individuals, who vex him by not going to a full length in transgression; and so he vents his rage on them, and exercises his cruelty, by letting them join the church of Christ with an unconverted heart, and compelling them, as the Jews did Simon, to bear the cross after Jesus. How sad this is; — to have no comfort in the pleasures of sin for a season; to be deprived of sinful gratifications in this life, with nothing to compensate for the deprivation here; and then to lie down in sorrow with the name and the recollections of one who once professedly bore the cross after Jesus.

There is another class of persons whose feelings are illustrated by those of Simon, if we may suppose him to have been apprehended against his will to bear the cross for Christ. They are some of those in a Christian congregation who are urged to become Christians, but are unwilling to repent and believe in the Saviour. Our efforts to make them the followers of Christ seem to them as unwelcome as did the approach of the Jewish officers and Roman soldiers to Simon, to make him bear the cross. To be a Christian seems to them to be like putting on them a most unwelcome, and a very heavy, burden. They have no heart for religion, nor for any of its spiritual truths, nor for any of its duties. If God will suffer them to go to heaven in their own way, they are willing to go; but to give up their sins, to submit to such humiliation and mortification as it would involve to be converted, is more than they can patiently endure. Probably, some of these persons cannot conceive of a more irksome condition than to be compelled to feel and act like Christians, with their present state of mind; and how to change this state of mind, or to make religion consistent with their feelings and tastes, is beyond their power to conceive. It is like compelling the Cyrenian to help Christ bear his cross. They look on those who would urge them to be followers of Christ and members of the church, as having a design against their happiness; perhaps as being selfish, over-zealous, and enthusiastic; and sometimes they congratulate themselves that they are able to withstand their persuasions, and are not deluded, like others, into a Christian profession. They associate with the idea of religion nothing which is pleasant; all is gloomy and repulsive; it is self-denial, mortification, perhaps pusillanimity; compared with which the pleasure of being their own masters, and the sense of independence in acting according to their own wishes, is bliss. If they should ever happen to be compelled, by affliction and sorrow, to become Christians, it seems to them that it will be no less a calamity than it was to this Simon to be caught by the mob and have his shoulders loaded with the hateful cross. It is nothing short of some terrible calamity, in their view, which can ever make them willing to be converted. If they should ever be so humbled and crushed by the hand of God as to be willing to be Christians, they suppose that they will submit to their fate. Looking on the procession that went with Christ to his crucifixion, there is no one, not even the innocent Jesus himself, for whom they, with their present feelings, would have had more sympathy, or whose feelings they would have appreciated or pitied more, than those of him who was caught and made cross-bearer to the Saviour of the world. They think that some have tried, in like manner, to put the cross on them; but they have escaped. When, in our solemn assemblies, the Saviour is, as it were, presented, on his way to Calvary, as, for example, in our sacramental lectures, and at the Lord's supper, they fear to expose themselves to the influences of such scenes, lest they should, in some way, be constrained, against their will, to take up the cross. We say these things with tender compassion, and not with reproachful feelings. We speak as those who have known the wormwood and the gall of an unrenewed and wicked heart.

We will turn to a more agreeable strain. Let us now suppose that Simon was a friend of Christ, and that his sons were disciples, and that the knowledge of these things led the Jews to lay the Saviour's cross upon him.

This being so, it is not impossible that Simon was on his way into the city to show his love and attach ment to his Saviour and Friend. Perhaps he had heard in the country the report of the Saviour's betrayal by one of his disciples, his apprehension, his mock trial, and the cruel treatment he had received from the populace. It may be that he, or some of his family, had been healed by Christ, or that Christ had forgiven his sins, and that he had become an heir of everlasting life. We can then imagine his feelings as he saw Christ in the hands of the mob, bleeding from the crown of thorns and from the scourging, bearing his cross without the gate to Calvary, and fainting under the load. His feeling may have been, O that I might die for him; O that they would take me, and release him, as they did Barabbas; O that I might be assisted to do something to show my love to Jesus. Perhaps these feelings were so evident that the people took advantage of them, and said, If you are such a friend and devotee of Christ, you surely will make no objection to carry his cross for him; and so, without further ceremony, "on him they laid the cross, that he might bear it after Jesus."

Here, then, we have this man again with the cross upon his shoulder; but a far different man is he from that which we have before supposed, and with far different feelings does he bear his load. What may we suppose his feelings to have been? Probably he was at that hour the happiest, and, in truth, the only happy, man in that crowd. The Saviour himself was exceeding sorrowful, even unto death; John, and Mary, and all the friends of Christ followed weeping; the wicked crew who were persecuting, and about to crucify, Christ, were not happy even in their exultation, for it was the laughter of fools. Simon may have been the only happy man in the whole crowd, and that because he was counted worthy to bear shame and reproach for Christ. It seems to him a providential kindness, that he was permitted to pass along the road just in time to meet Christ and the multitude; just in time to lift this dreadful burden from the Saviour, and have it laid on his own neck. He goes forward with it with more joy than though he were an honored attendant of Cæsar in a triumphal procession. He would rather bear the cross after Christ than the royal train for the emperor. The people around him, it may be, mock him, and call him a friend of the malefactor, and, in many ways, insult him under his burden; but to all their provocations and jeers he makes no answer, except it be a prayer, Lord, that their eyes may be opened. They tell him, perhaps, that he will always be known, hereafter, as the man that had the Nazarene's cross laid on his shoulders, on the way to Golgotha. If he is really a friend of Jesus, he esteems the reproach of Christ greater riches than the treasures of Egypt.

"If on my face, for thy dear name,
Shame and reproaches be,
I'll hail reproach, and welcome shame,
If thou remember me."

He knows but little, with all his joy, he yet knows but little of the honor that is put upon him. What is that cross to be? It is the altar for the Lamb of God that taketh away the sin of the world. That cross is the instrument of our redemption from hell, and Simon bore it for us, and all the redeemed in heaven will feel that he was their friend in helping on that cross to Calvary. What would Simon, in heaven, take in exchange for the honor and privilege of having borne that cross after Jesus? You could not purchase it of him with an earthly throne; you could not make him feel that any disciple of Christ on the earth, or any martyr since his time, has more to make him happy than he has in his recollections of the hour when he bore the cross after Jesus. What happiness will that man enjoy forever. As the redeemed, of all ages and nations, think over and rehearse to one another the history of the cross, they will remember the man, however humble and obscure he may have been, that man of Cyrene, that African, who was so highly honored as to be a copartner with Emmanuel in the labor of carrying the cross to the mount of sacrifice. Happy, happy man! You may respond to Paul's exultation: "God forbid that I should glory, save in the cross of our Lord Jesus Christ." Not that there was any merit in the act, to justify his soul; not that the piece of wood had any virtue in it more than any other tree; but because the grace of God enabled him to show his faithful love to the Saviour by this act, and to be associated with that which is the instrument of a world's salvation, and of his own.

One practical truth is well illustrated by this narrative: —

OUR FEELINGS MAKE RELIGION, AND EVERY THING CONNECTED WITH IT, EASY OR DIFFICULT, PLEASANT OR REPULSIVE.

We know that this principle holds good in common things; in our business and professions, in labors and sacrifices. Love impels us to every kind action; we feel no burden, no sacrifice, where love reigns in the heart. A parent, a husband, a wife, or child, will labor and suffer for a beloved object in forms and to a degree, which no wealth could induce them to do or to bear for one whom they did not love, or for a stranger. We can all enter into the feelings of Simon in bearing this cross, if he were a truly good man and an ardent friend of Christ; we know that, if we felt toward the Saviour, or toward any friend, as he may have done, nothing could give us greater joy than to perform such an act as his. Let the multitude sneer and insult; let hell join with earth to mock us; love to the injured and suffering Friend would bear us on, and make us more than conquerors, through Him that loved us.

Religion is the highest joy, or the greatest affliction, according to the state of our feelings toward God and spiritual things.

If we love the world, and our sins, and worldly company; if we hanker after sinful pleasures and vain amusements; if we dislike prayer, and the Bible, and self-denial, and contemplations on death and heaven, and feel no interest in doing good to the souls, but only to the bodies, of men, — of course religion is a great hardship. If we profess religion, we then wish we had never done so; and if we are not, professedly, Christians, nothing is more unwelcome than the thought of being such. So that religion is to every one of us, without exception, just what the cross of Christ was to Simon, in one of the states of mind in which we have supposed him to be.

Now, if any one of us is sorry that he ever professed to be a Christian, and thinks that he is not one, and would be glad to be released from his obligations, we would say, Your only hope of happiness and safety, here and hereafter, and the only relief for you from your present embarrassment, lies in your becoming a faithful follower and friend of your

Redeemer. As for escaping from your vows to God, which your lips have uttered, and which your soul made when you were in trouble, you cannot do it. If you should receive a letter signed by your pastor, the office-bearers, and the members of the church, releasing you from the church, you might feel relieved for a while; but that letter would soon be to you a heavier burden than poor Simon bore, if, with unwilling neck, he endured the reproach of Christ. On a dying bed, that letter would seem to you, in your dreams and visions, like a great gate, shutting you out of heaven. What a sight it would be, to see you before the Lord your Judge, with that letter in your hand. It would be the last thing which you would take with you to the bar of God; but suppose that you should be summoned to appear with the letter, and it should be read before the Judge, thus: "This certifies that —— is, at his (or her) own request, this day released from covenant obligations to God and the Lord Jesus, and is no more a member of the Saviour's visible church, which is his body." Pastors are sometimes requested to procure a letter of release for some from the church of Christ. What would induce them to put their names to such a letter, to be read before Christ, and so to stand in the place of your last, dread sentence, as to make it needless that Christ should say unto you, Depart?

No, dear friend, who have lost your interest in religion, ensnared with the fascinations of this present evil world, or who have, by some unhappy means, left your first love to Christ, and on whose shoulders the cross is heavy, too heavy for you to bear; to whom will you go, if you go from Christ? The Saviour speaks to you as he did to Simon Peter: "Satan hath desired to have thee, that he may sift thee as wheat; but I have prayed for thee, that thy faith may not fail." You know that religion is of intrinsic importance, though you think you never felt its power; now, the same almighty grace which has given to others 'a new heart,' and 'a new spirit,' can do this for you. Repentance, and faith in the blood of Jesus Christ, will be as efficacious in your case as in theirs. Personal religion, or Christian character, is not like a garment which is spoiled when made, without remedy. Therefore do not cast off your Christian profession, and say that you are a hypocrite in professing that which you do not feel. Keep your Christian profession, and conform to it, by obtaining grace from him who "upbraideth not." It seems that you must bear the cross, willingly or unwillingly; Christ will gently lay it on you, or the world, knowing what you have professed, will thrust it upon you. But Christ says, My yoke is easy, and my burden is light. Was it heavy and galling to the pious and faithful Simon? Even you may obtain those feelings which will make the cross of Christ your joy and your crown.

It would be in vain for an unconverted man to think of being happy, as a Christian, while he retains his love of the world and sin. No wonder that religion is uninviting to him, and the service of Christ a cross from which he flies, so long as he is conscious of no love to Christ. But religion does not take your pleasures from you, and give you nothing in exchange. On the contrary, it substitutes for your poor, unsatisfying pleasures, joys which, once tasted, will make your worldly joys distasteful. Begin to love the Saviour who loved you, and, in the same sense, loves you still. Then we shall put no cross upon you, in bringing you into his kingdom; but that which others consider a cross, you will esteem your glory and your crown.

While we live here, with these natures but partly sanctified, we shall always have to bear some cross, if we would live holy, and righteously, and godly, in this present evil world. May we, instead of shunning the cross, be willing to walk so near to Christ that we could (as some interpret Simon's bearing the cross "after Jesus") feel and bear one end of his cross on our necks, and, instead of fearing reproach, and seeking for reputation and pleasure in the world, plant our feet in his very footsteps, though they lead to Calvary, taking part with him, despised and rejected of men, and, if need be, 'filling up that which is behind of the afflictions of Christ for his body's sake, which is the church.' No man ever had a nearer and sweeter union with Christ than the man who, willingly and joyfully, bore the cross which was taken from the Saviour's neck, and laid on him. We may question whether it were not a greater honor, and is not now a greater happiness, to Simon, if in heaven, to have been thus joined to Christ by his cross, than it was, or is, to the beloved disciple merely to have leaned on his breast. Who would not as willingly be Simon, with the Saviour's cross, as John upon the Saviour's bosom?

Of the two pictures which have been drawn of Simon, one of them corresponds to the character and feelings of each of us, in our public and private life. If we are not fugitives from the cross, and from Christ, as he may have tried to be, we are compelled to keep up the profession of a Christian, feeling unhappy, and looking this way and that to escape; or, if a picture could be made of us, it would represent us as coming to Christ, offering ourselves to be the partners of his shame and of his cause. We almost envy some who have the opportunity to make a sacrifice of feeling and worldly interest in becoming Christians. If Simon the Cyrenian is with Christ in heaven, we would all of us give the whole world, could we do so, for his joy, and for that love which

Christ bears him. He who turned his back toward him on the way to Calvary, and suffered him to bear his cross, now turns his face on him with a smile which is a heaven in Heaven.

Do not wait till it is easier for you, as you suppose it may hereafter be, to become a Christian. That might be an irreparable loss, and, when Christ distributes our last rewards, an occasion for great regret. Come then, take up your cross. "Jesus, also, that he might sanctify the people with his own blood, suffered without the gate. LET US GO FORTH, THEREFORE, UNTO HIM WITHOUT THE CAMP, BEARING HIS REPROACH. FOR HERE HAVE WE NO CONTINUING CITY, BUT WE SEEK ONE TO COME." And, "IF WE SUFFER, WE SHALL ALSO REIGN WITH HIM."

SERMON X.

THE PENITENT THIEF.

LUKE XXIII. 42, 43.

AND HE SAID UNTO JESUS, LORD, REMEMBER ME WHEN THOU COMEST INTO THY KINGDOM. AND JESUS SAID UNTO HIM, VERILY I SAY UNTO THEE, TO-DAY SHALT THOU BE WITH ME IN PARADISE.

THE three crosses which stood together on Mount Calvary, are a continual emblem of our world. A dying Saviour had, on one side of him, an enemy and unbeliever, and on the other side, a friend and believer. Thus it is to-day in every part of the globe where Christ is preached; thus it is in every Christian congregation.

This narrative is an instance of those discrepancies which we find in the several accounts of the same events by the different evangelists. One of them says, "The thieves which were crucified with him cast the same in his teeth," that is, the same reproaches with the scribes: 'If thou be the Christ, save thyself.' But another evangelist represents that only one of the thieves upbraided Christ; and therefore some are disposed to reflect upon the accuracy and trustworthiness of the sacred penmen.

The discrepancy is satisfactorily explained in either of two ways. 1. It is a common method of speaking to use the plural number, when only one of a multitude may have been intended. We have an instance of the same kind in the story of the alabaster box of ointment. "And they that sat at meat with him had indignation, saying, To what purpose is this waste?" But another evangelist says that this remark was made by Judas Iscariot; and his motives are given. All that one of the evangelists wished to intimate was, that fault was found at table with this precious gift; while the other historian enters into particulars. We use the same method of speaking. If a mob surrounds a house, and we say, They threw stones, this would be true, though but one man threw them. The idea is, stones were thrown; and this mode of speech is deemed sufficiently accurate in a general narrative, while, in a court of justice, the narrator might be required to tell whether he saw more than one man commit the outrage. So, one evangelist merely notices, in passing, the affecting circumstance that Jesus, in the agonies of crucifixion, received insult from among the two who were themselves dying by crucifixion. Even they who were crucified with him contributed to his sufferings. This is sufficiently accurate for the purpose.

But there is another way of explaining and reconciling this discrepancy. 2. It is possible that, at the first, both of the thieves did join to insult Christ. Who will undertake to say that they did not, or to deny that one of them afterward relented, and took the Saviour's part against his fellow?

Many interesting and important truths are illustrated by this narrative.

I. THE HISTORY OF THE PENITENT THIEF IS A STRIKING ILLUSTRATION OF FAITH.

There are two remarkable expressions in the brief prayer which he addressed to Christ, both of them exhibiting wonderful faith. One is, "thy kingdom." Thy kingdom!—as though the suffering, dying Jesus had a kingdom. This idea was a subject of sport and ridicule below, while on the cross it was an object of faith. Above the cross, even Pilate writes a caricature: "This is Jesus of Nazareth, the King of the Jews." To let every man of every tongue in that motley crowd have his chance to understand the criminal pretensions of Jesus, this accusation was written in Hebrew, and Greek, and Latin. But let the Hebrews, and the Greeks, and the Romans, with Pilate at their head—let the whole priesthood, and all the scribes—insult at the idea of that crucified victim having a kingdom; nevertheless, this poor thief speaks to the Saviour of his "kingdom." Numbers, rank, laughter, jests, nails, and spears, have no effect on him. His faith is like Mount Zion, which cannot be moved. It was a singular word, indeed, that ascended amid the hellish revelry around the cross, addressed to him who was despised and rejected of men, — "When thou comest into thy kingdom."

What evidence had this penitent thief that Christ had a kingdom? What did he know which was not known to his fellow on the other side of Christ? Absolutely nothing. Yet we hear him expressing his faith in Jesus as being all which he professed to be. His ideas were necessarily vague with regard to Christ's kingdom, but his faith was nevertheless genuine faith.

What a reproof this is to unbelief — the unbelief of those who, with all the accumulated evidence which a Christian education affords, still say that they cannot bring themselves to believe. Surely unbelief is not always owing to a want of evidence; nor is faith always proportioned to evidence; for the penitent thief had, in the circumstances of the case, very little warrant for his belief. What, then, is the explanation of such faith? It is simply this: his heart was touched; his feelings were disposed to look favorably on Christ. So true it is, as the inspired word declares, that "with the heart man believeth unto righteousness." Where the feelings are inclined toward any view of the case, it is easy to refute, in our own minds, accusations made against beloved objects, and to see excellences where others see only faults.

In religion, the great difficulty with all who are not deficient in knowledge, and yet do not believe, is, they have no heart for it. That which we dislike, it is comparatively easy to disprove, or, at least, to heap up objections to it.

This gives us an affecting view of unbelief in religion, as criminal. It is not a mere dissatisfaction with evidence; for there is evidence enough in religion — evidence which has convinced the most prejudiced, the most learned, the most ignorant. But one says, I am not responsible for them, nor they for me. What if all the world are satisfied with certain evidence; must I believe merely because they believe? Certainly not; but we have reason, in such a case, to inquire, whether the fault lies most in the head or the heart; that is, whether we are so dull that we cannot reason as well as the rest of the world, or whether a deceived heart has turned us aside.

We see, then, why it is that belief and unbelief are subjects of reward and punishment. It would not be just to say, 'He that believeth shall be saved, and he that believeth not shall be damned,' unless a man's heart, his will, were concerned in the unbelief, as they are in every case. Many a man is fortifying himself against the claims of religion, on the ground that his mind cannot receive certain truths; whereas it is not because the evidence is defective; for, should he meet with affliction, or, in some way, be humbled, so that his feelings should be changed, his perplexities would be cleared up, showing that the difficulty is not with the evidence, but in the state of the heart. It is also said, "He that doeth evil hateth the light, neither cometh to the light, that his deeds may be reproved." So that the common declaration, I am not responsible for my belief, is not true, because in religion, where there is sufficient knowledge, our belief is determined by our feelings; if we feel right, we believe aright. It was so with the penitent thief. The silent Sufferer by his side affected his subdued heart with relentings, and with sympathy; while the effect on the hard heart of the other thief, was, to make him upbraid Christ.

The other expression in the penitent thief's prayer, which expresses his faith, is this: "Lord, remember me." The other words, "thy kingdom," expressed a general belief in Christ. These words, "Remember me," were the triumph of faith. Grant that Christ has a kingdom, and is on his way to his throne; it would have been natural for the thief to have been overawed by the thought of that dying Potentate, and to have feared to make any request of him. Yet he prefers this request: "Lord, remember me." He was not, in his own esteem, too wicked, and too far below the notice of Christ; though he had the worst possible thoughts of himself as a malefactor, who received the due reward of his deeds in being crucified. What boldness, and 'confidence of access, by the faith of him,' did this poor creature have, in thus appealing to Christ. See in it a perfect illustration of faith, which cannot be explained, or made any more forcible, by words. It is hung up by the side of the very cross of Christ, that if any wish to know what faith in Christ is, and whether they can be forgiven, and whether they are not too wicked, and too unworthy to hope for the favor of God, they have the answer, recorded in the most conspicuous place of all the earth; not in St. Peter's Cathedral, nor at the side of the highways, but by the cross of Jesus. It stands, the most perfect illustration of the way to believe in Christ, and a refutation of the error that believing and not believing depend on the amount of evidence, and a rebuke of the pride which keeps many a sinner, conscious of guilt, from asking for mercy.

Once more look at this picture: there is another feature which we have not noticed, another illustration of the faith in the dying thief. "Remember me," he cries, — not merely now, but "when thou comest into thy kingdom." He might, by great faith, have asked Christ to help him die easily, to forgive his sins; but, while all this is included, we are astonished at the reach and grasp of this man's faith. Will Christ have nothing to do, or to think of? When Jesus comes in his kingly majesty, will he, can he, spend time or thought, then, on a poor, crucified thief? Is not this presumption, pretending to ask for a remembrance amid the glory and honor of the coronation day? Was there ever such faith as this? Did not Jesus rebuke it? He seems to forget his own dying agonies, to applaud and reward such faith, promising that, that very day, this man should be with him in paradise.

Let us never say, I cannot believe. Or, if we cannot, let us go with the hearts which keep us from believing, and, at the cross of Christ, take a lesson from that dying malefactor. It does not appear that, up to the time when Christ replied to his prayer, the Saviour had said one word to him. Christ had not looked to those malefactors for sympathy. While he, notwithstanding his own sufferings, must have felt compassion for them, it might not have been of good effect for him to speak with them at such an hour; for his enemies would have misunderstood his motives, and might have said, He has fellow-feeling with malefactors. There was propriety, and wisdom too, in this — that when he was brought as a lamb to the slaughter, as a sheep before her shearers he was dumb; he opened not his mouth. We find no evidence of the common and natural appeal from him which companions in misery, though strangers, make to each other for sympathy.

Bearing the burden of the world's atonement; tasting death for every man; finishing, by the last act of suffering and dying, the work of propitiation; fulfilling, in that hour, all that Moses and the prophets had written, — he stands, with two thieves, in one group, waiting each to be nailed to his respective cross. O Saviour, we are glad that at that hour there was one who spoke for some of us, and expressed the feelings of penitent sinners in all ages, and took thy part, and witnessed a good confession. He puts us to shame by his wonderful faith. How timid and slow we are to commit our souls to thee, while this poor thief spake to thee, hanging on the cross, of thy kingdom, and asked thee to remember him — to remember him amid the glories of thy kingdom. Paul's faith, at his conversion, was not so great as this. Christ spoke to him from heaven. The penitent thief spoke first to Christ. "Blessed are they that have not seen, and yet have believed."

Perhaps some will say, Would that I could have just such faith as this: why may I not have it? how can I obtain it?

It may be, if Christ had not done so much for you, it might have been easier to believe in him. He has knocked at the door of your heart ever since you were a child; he has spared you, and interceded for you, and blessed you; he has followed you with the means of salvation, employing ministers to plead his love for you, and his willingness to forgive you and save you. All this he has done, and you ask, Why may I not believe in Christ, and have strong faith in him? A question more easily answered is one like these: What guilt, without excuse, is mine, to have rejected Christ, with the accumulated evidence of his Godhead, and of his sufferings for me? Who is a greater sinner than I, to have treated the Saviour as I have done? How can I stand in the judgment, if I plead that I did not know how to believe in Christ, especially if the penitent thief should be permitted to ask me there, In what way do you suppose that I, a dying thief, knew what it was to believe in Christ?

II. The history of the penitent thief illustrates the nature of free grace in Jesus Christ.

Grace is favor to the guilty, and of course to the undeserving. It never had a more vivid illustration than in the case before us.

The closing act of the Saviour's life was the salvation of a sinner. While earth and hell were triumphing over his supposed defeat, he rescued an immortal spirit from hell, and thus carried into effect the object of his death, even while he was dying.

But who is he that is selected as the subject of this victorious grace, at such a moment? All heaven are intently watching that scene; the redeemed look down upon that cross with feelings of unutterable interest. They are waiting to receive the soul of Jesus as it passes from earth to heaven; and behold, a spirit passes up, also, to heaven from the side of Christ. And who is it? The Emperor of Rome, perhaps, or the high priest; the beloved disciple, or Mary the mother of Jesus. It is the soul of a thief, taken from prison and adjudged to an ignominious death; he is the companion of Jesus in death, and in his entrance into heaven.

This is characteristic of Christ and of divine grace. Here was a dying malefactor. The sorrows of death gat hold upon him, and the pains of hell compassed him about. He found trouble and sorrow. Then called he upon the name of the Lord: O Lord, I beseech thee, deliver my soul. The faithful saying is verified, and is worthy of all acceptation, that Christ Jesus came into the world to save sinners — even the chief. We are glad that it was not an emperor, nor a disciple, it is so beautiful an illustration of grace. We can understand it further by supposing what the feelings of that thief must have been at finding himself in heaven. A few hours before, he was in prison, awaiting death for his crimes. Now he is before the throne of God, now he is in the presence of just men made perfect, now he hears joy in the presence of the angels of God over him.

What must have been his strange joy as he looked round in heaven, and with what feelings afterward must he have regarded that Saviour who delivered him from the wrath to come.

Such is grace; and every one of us — strange as some may think it — every one of us, if saved, will be saved in the same way; every one of us who are saved, will vie with that penitent thief to show that we owe as much to Christ as he. We shall, perhaps, contest his claims to preëminence as a subject of wonderful grace; for many of us will say to him, You were forgiven and saved without ever having heard of and rejected Christ. We lived till we were ten or twelve years old, or twenty, or forty, or sixty, rejecting that Saviour on whom you believed the first time that you heard him. Did you, O penitent thief, ever turn your back on the body and blood of Christ offered to you? We did, for years. Did you live in known sin, for years, rejecting the offer of redeeming love? Were you ever at the point of death, by accident or sickness; and, being snatched from death, did you go on rejecting Christ? Did you have a seat in a Christian temple, pious parents, meetings for religious inquiry, Bibles, the Holy Spirit striving with you, all in vain — for years in vain? Take away that crown, O penitent thief, which you have cast at Jesus' feet as the crown of one who owes most to the grace of God; to mine, as much as to yours, belongs that great distinction, and let it have, at least, an equal place there. Here, Saviour, is the crown of a redeemed sinner, from a Christian land, in the nineteenth century — a sinner against light and love unparalleled, spared and forgiven, and saved from a hell which would have been more tolerable for thieves, and for Sodom, than for me.

The penitent thief did no more and no less than men now do when they come to Christ. He came just as he was. He did not wait to feel more — to know that Christ would receive him before he came to him; he did not complain that he was convinced but not persuaded; he did not wish to make himself better before he applied to Christ; he came to Christ in all his vileness, and cast himself upon the Saviour's mercy. Precisely so do sinners now come to the Saviour, — just as they are. Their appropriate language is, —

> "The dying thief rejoiced to see
> That fountain in his day;
> And there have I, as vile as he,
> Washed all my sins away." *

There is not one way of salvation, therefore, for the penitent thief, and another for us. He, and the jailer at Philippi, and the three thousand at Pentecost, and all others, are saved in the same way. "For other foundation can no man lay than that is laid, which is Jesus Christ." "For by grace are we

* Thus Cowper wrote it. See Grimshaw's Cowper.

saved through faith; and that not of yourselves; — it is the gift of God."

Let it be borne in mind, then, for without it this subject, and the case in Scripture on which it is founded, will have no useful influence upon us — that this method of saving the thief was nothing strange. He was not saved in one way, and we in another. The only peculiarity in his case was, that so late, and with such small evidence as he enjoyed, he should have been saved. But he was saved precisely as we shall be, if we are saved; on the very same principles, and for the same reasons; that is to say, renouncing all merit, and trusting only and wholly to Christ. The most virtuous man has no more merit before Christ than that thief. "All our righteousnesses (that is, the things which we set up as meritorious, or grounds of claim) are as filthy rags," and, in the sight of God, as filthy as those of the thief. If you are saved, you must be saved, not, perhaps, as a penitent thief, but as a penitent —— How shall we fill the blank? A large blank will be required, for "who can understand his errors?" Even Job said, "How many are mine iniquities and sins? Make me to know my transgression and my sin." We must each be saved by mercy to the lost and perishing; and the penitent thief was no more lost and perishing than we are, except that his dying hour had actually come.

III. The case of the penitent thief is a warning to those who defer repentance.

If we should see a man who went over the falls of Niagara in a boat, and was saved, should it encourage us to venture into the rapids? What a risk this thief ran; how near he came to losing that heaven which he has now secured. Here is the only case in the Bible of repentance at the close of life. One instance is given, that none may despair; and only one, that none may presume.

Some think that sickness and suffering will arouse them. But stupidity in religion is voluntary. It is not like being frozen or stunned. Stupidity in religion is voluntary. No one need be stupid; no one is stupid who does his known duty.

As to the effect of suffering to arouse and persuade, look on the other side of Christ upon the cross. Suffering hardens as frequently as it softens. The probability is extremely small that a man who has all his lifetime known his duty and neglected religion, will come to his senses in death. Men generally die as they live. God agrees to no such proposal as this: — I will repent at the last hour. He sometimes says, "Because I have called and ye have refused, I also will laugh at your calamity, I will mock when your fear cometh."

A sick man is afraid to prepare to die, because that is an admission to his own mind, that he may not, or will not, recover; so he puts it off till it is too late. Disease has wasted him; wandering thoughts and weakness of mind frequently prevent him from saying or doing any thing that requires the least effort: the little child must not be brought into the room, for its bright face is too exciting; and if you lift a bunch of flowers to his eye, even that sight disturbs him, and he involuntarily wishes you to let him alone. Think of trying to do, in such a moment, that which for years, in health and full strength, a man has complained that he could not undertake, or do. "If thou hast run with the footmen, and they have wearied thee, then how canst thou contend with horses? and if in the land of peace, wherein thou trustedst, they wearied thee, then how wilt thou do in the swellings of Jordan?" Even if we could be saved at the last hour, what treatment is this of God our Saviour, to give him the miserable remnant of a misspent life. Some are of the opinion that this thief was penitent before he went to the cross. If so, there is not even one instance in the Bible of true repentance in the dying hour. There is great kindness, as well as solemn admonition, in the words of the Holy Ghost: "To-day, if ye will hear his voice, harden not your hearts." This is followed by saying that 'he limiteth a certain day.' The meaning is, the offers of pardon are made on condition of their being accepted at the time. They do not include to-morrow.

IV. THE CASE OF THE THIEF IS A PROOF OF INSTANTANEOUS RETRIBUTION AFTER DEATH.

We learn from Paul's account of his being caught up into the third heaven, or, as he says in a subsequent verse, into paradise, that paradise is the third heaven. It certainly is the place where the Saviour spent the interval between death and the resurrection. Can any Protestant believe that he spent it elsewhere than in the heaven of heavens?

There is no reason to suppose that departed souls are in a state of happiness inferior to that which they will enjoy after the resurrection, except that the addition of the body will contribute greatly to their happiness, and make, perhaps, the difference of gazing for a time, in full health and strength, at the starry heavens, enjoying the sight in the company of intelligent friends; and afterward possessing the advantages of a telescope. The telescope is an addition to your means of enjoyment, but not to your character, or consciousness. The Westminster Assembly's Shorter Catechism expresses the scriptural truth: "The souls of believers are, at their death, made perfect in holiness, and do immediately pass into glory; their bodies, being still united to Christ, do rest in their graves until the resurrection."

If so, how near the Christian is, continually, to his home in heaven. A sudden accident, a sharp, short sickness may dismiss his spirit, and immediately it takes 'its mansion near the throne.' Suppose that there were, in a certain room of your house, a company of angels who were waiting to convey you to heaven, and you knew it. What manner of persons would you be in all holy conversation and godliness? We ought to live, continually, seeing that we look for these things, in such a manner that we may, at any time, "be found of him in peace, without spot, and blameless."

It is also true that sinners are, in like manner, living on the very brink of hell. A blow, a fall, a sudden sickness, may launch them forth into eternity, and all is over with them forever. We are dividing, every day, or week, or month, like the two on the cross, on either side of Christ; and each of us will follow one or the other of them, to his paradise or to his punishment. Some are crying, "Lord, remember me"; some are perishing at the side of Christ. He who hung at Christ's side, but reviled him, will think forever: 'What an opportunity I had, with my fellow, to be saved, at the very side of Jesus.' Like him, some one who reads these lines may often have said, with a complaining feeling, If thou be the Christ, save me; why have I never found pardon, when I have asked for it so long? "Dost thou not fear God, seeing thou art" justly "in a state of condemnation?" When you feel this, you will acquit Christ of all blame at his delay, saying, This man hath done nothing amiss; but this man (smiting your breast) hath done every thing amiss.

Finally, it would be doing injustice to the subject, if the closing impression should not be made by the truth illustrated so strikingly by this narrative, namely: —

V. Christ is able and willing to save great sinners.

He illustrated this in three remarkable ways: —

On the cross, while making the atonement, he manifested his power and willingness to save great sinners, by saving a dying thief.

After he had risen from the dead, he told his disciples to offer pardon to men in his name, 'beginning at Jerusalem.' Go, first of all, to my crucifiers; tell them that I loved them, and gave myself for them. This was actually done; and many believed, and were saved. Once more:

When he selected an apostle to the Gentile world, he chose one who was a persecutor, a blasphemer, and injurious, and made him a pattern of what he was able and willing to do in the case of great transgressors. We hear that convert say, "This is a faithful saying, and worthy of all acceptation, that Christ Jesus came into the world to save sinners, of whom I am chief. Howbeit, for this cause I obtained mercy, that in me first Jesus Christ might show forth a pattern to all who should hereafter believe on him to life everlasting." The greatness of guilt, then, is no reason, in itself, why it may not be forgiven. "Wherefore he is able also to save them to the uttermost that come unto God by him, seeing that he ever liveth to make intercession for them."

We shall each see a time when the prayer of the penitent thief will seem to us the most appropriate to our case. Christ is coming into his kingdom; coming, in his own glory, and in the glory of the Father, and of the holy angels. 'Every eye shall see him.' While the heavens are on fire, the elements melting, the graves opening, the risen dead preparing to ascend to judgment, and the Son of man is throned above the clouds, is there a petition that you would love to have answered more than this—Lord, remember me? Could you, by any means, induce Christ to remember you at such a time, and obtain from him a token of favor, what would you not give? You can secure a remembrance of yourself then. The way to do it is, to remember him now. Remember him, in the midst of your follies, and worldliness, and sins, and give yourself to him. Remember him, while you ask, What must I do to be saved? and commit yourself to him, like this thief. Remember him at his table; for he has said, 'Do this in remembrance of me.' Remember him in your temptations, and keep his word.

Remember him always, as your Example, Guide, Friend, and Saviour. "For every one that seeth the Son, and believeth on him, hath everlasting life; and I will raise him up at the last day."

SERMON XI.

THE RELENTING CRUCIFIER.

MATT. XXVII. 48.

AND STRAIGHTWAY ONE OF THEM RAN, AND TOOK A SPONGE, AND FILLED IT WITH VINEGAR, AND PUT IT ON A REED, AND GAVE HIM TO DRINK.

AMONG the friends of Christ, we find a relenting crucifier. In companies where we should least expect it God secures witnesses for himself; and in hearts which appear to be the most unpromising soil we find the work of the Spirit.

The act performed by this partner of the crucifixion was so very slight, and evinces so little interest in Christ, that his claim to a place among the friends of Christ may naturally be questioned. It is not with the expectation of proving his claim, by any argument founded on his cursory act of kindness, that he is here included in the number of the Saviour's friends; but for the purpose of showing that the infinite condescension of the Saviour, in recognizing a cup of cold water given to one of his disciples in the name of a disciple, as worthy of his reward, and in sparing a bruised reed, and treating with forbearance and hopefulness the smoking flax, may have found an object of grace even among those who were employed to bruise him and put him to grief. It may encourage some to see how slight a feeling of interest in Christ, how inconsiderable an act of kindness done for him, may bring a man within the wide circumference of that grace which rejoices in showing mercy where sin has abounded, nor is turned away from scenes the most revolting and hopeless to the eye of our faith. Besides, if all who befriended Christ were endowed with great talents, or were in affluent circumstances, or if all of them belonged to the intelligent classes of society, or even if they all enjoyed and exercised clear and strong faith, it is easy to see that very many might be discouraged. By including the penitent thief and the relenting crucifier in the number of the Saviour's friends, we feel sure that we act in accordance with the spirit of that "faithful saying, worthy of all acceptation, that Christ Jesus came into the world to save sinners," "and that the Son of man came to seek and to save that which is lost."

Crucifixion always occasioned an intolerable thirst. To make the victims insensible, stupefying drinks were humanely offered. Christ refused such a draught, and died with an unclouded mind. His followers may innocently receive alleviations of pain, and use them, even to the suspension of their consciousness, if they choose, or their friends so determine for them; but the manner in which Christ chose to meet death, illustrates the common reflection of suffering Christians, that their pains are not to be compared with those which Christ endured on their account; while it should serve to strengthen them for "all patience and long-suffering with joyfulness."

The dreadful scenes and agonies of the cross drew near their end. The last act of the Saviour's life was to commend his mother to the beloved disciple, who was standing near the cross, and who thus continues the account of the scene: "After this, Jesus, knowing that all things were now accomplished, that the Scriptures might be fulfilled, saith, I thirst."

The seeming digression will not be found inconsistent with unity of effect, if we consider here the wonderful minuteness with which the sufferings of Christ were foretold, and their extreme coincidence with the predictions.

As soon as Christ was nailed to the cross, the soldiers, rapacious and poor, seized upon his garments, which his crucifiers had stripped from him, and as there were four of these soldiers, probably, who were detailed to attend the execution, they apportioned his garments between them; his coat, making a fifth portion, consisting of one piece of cloth, without a seam, fell to one of them by lot.

Who but Omniscience could have foreseen that little incident of division, and the casting of the lot, in the distribution of the Saviour's garments? What a wonderful book the Bible appears to be; the more wonderful, the more minutely it is examined. God is in it, as in nature, wherever the eye rests or penetrates.

With respect to the manner in which the bodies of the three victims on those crosses were treated, there is the same remarkable fulfilment of prophecy. The Jews were unwilling that the bodies of men crucified should remain on the cross during the Sabbath; indeed, it was their custom always to remove a crucified body from the cross before sundown; but the near approach of the Sabbath, beginning at six o'clock of the preceding afternoon, made them anxious to dispose of the bodies without delay. They therefore begged the Roman governor, that the usual mode of hastening death might be resorted to; viz., a violent breaking of the legs of the victims. By this means, the two thieves were hastened out of the world. When they came to Christ to do the same, they found that he was already dead. Whether his death took place before the thieves had, either or both of them, died, does not appear; but, at least, when they were dead, it was found that he was dead, and they therefore brake not his legs.

In this apparently simple incident we find a proof of Christ's atoning sacrifice, as our passover slain for us. Among the directions for offering and eating the passover lamb, this is given: "Neither shall ye break a bone thereof." It was to be eaten in haste, while the family stood round the table, girded for a journey, with their shoes upon them, and their staves in their hands. They must not wait to break the bones; and the delay which it would occasion was the immediate, the obvious, reason for that commandment.

But there was a deeper reason why the limbs of Christ should not be broken. That body must not be mutilated in one degree more than the necessities of crucifixion required. That body was to ascend into heaven; it must preserve its perfectness, except so far as the instruments of death should fix their prints in it. The breaking of any of the limbs of Christ would forever have conveyed to the mind the idea of weakness, which would subtract from certain associations which it seemed desirable should be connected with his body. He must be 'crucified in weakness;' but no needless indignity must be offered to his person. Therefore a bone of him must not be broken. He was not set to honor the paschal lamb; but the paschal lamb was appointed to honor him, and therefore, that the passover lamb might be like Christ, it was ordered that the Israelites should not break one of its bones. Again we are struck with the wonderful character of the Bible, in its minute points. While the thieves had their bones broken, it was appointed that the Saviour should not need it to hasten his death; and so he escaped this indignity, and thus fulfilled the type of the lamb at the passover.

But to make it certain that he was dead, a soldier, having a spear, thrust it into his side, "and forthwith there came out blood and water." This, according to the testimony of medical men, would have produced death, had he not been already dead; — the mingled blood and water coming from the region of the heart, where the spear had pierced. Again, another scripture saith, 'They shall look on him whom they have pierced!'

All these prophecies were familiar to Christ, and the knowledge of them bore him through his sufferings until they were finished. One suffering, one pang only, remained; one prophetic touch in the picture of his agony, alone, was yet to be fulfilled. "Jesus, knowing that all things were now accomplished, that the Scriptures might be fulfilled, said, I thirst."

This was necessary to prove that his sufferings were the ordinary sufferings of the cross. Had there been no thirst, as there always was in other cases, the inference would have been that he did not suffer, but was supported and relieved by supernatural power, and so did not "bear our sins in his own body on the tree." But that cup must not pass from him except he drink it. The sufferings of Christ are portrayed by David. Among them we read: "In my thirst, they gave me vinegar to drink." Jesus said, "I thirst." It was an involuntary outcry; crucifixion was draining every nerve and fibre of its natural moisture; and that suffering, probably the greatest of which the human body is capable, the suffering occasioned by thirst, compared with which the pains of hunger are slight, made him cry with a pitiable distress.

That cry struck to the heart of one of them that stood by, participating in the bloody deed. There stood by the cross a vessel filled with the common drink of the Roman soldiers, called 'posca,' or sour wine, which, when mixed with water, was a palatable acid. It was one of the preparations for crucifixion to place that liquid by the cross. This relenting crucifier ran, and filled a sponge with it, and fixing it on a reed, or a stalk of the hyssop, reached it to the Saviour's dying and parched lips. Christ had refused the wine and myrrh; he would not be made insensible to his sufferings; but he was willing to receive this act of kindness, and when he had tasted the vinegar, he said, It is finished, and he bowed his head, and gave up the ghost. It would seem that the restlessness of dying had come over his exhausted system; the rending asunder of soul and body was taking place; the cooling, grateful taste of the vinegar gave him, as it were, a little strength to die, excited a pleasurable sensation which itself exhausted his remaining strength; as we often see a patient die instantly, after being lifted a little in his bed, or turned on his pillow. With a feeling of relief, he uttered those words whose meaning is coextensive with the whole plan of salvation, from the foundation of the world: "It is finished." In that moment, "he tasted death for every man."

He who performed the last act of kindness which the Saviour of the world received before his death, was by no means a believer, as we learn from the account of him by Mark. While he was performing this act of kindness, Matthew says, "The rest said, Let be; let us see whether Elias will come to save him." This is erroneously understood as a prohibition: Do not give him the vinegar; let Elias relieve him if he will. That this is not the meaning, appears from Mark, who makes the man himself utter these words. Mark says, "And one ran, and filled a sponge with vinegar, and put it on a reed, and gave him to drink, saying, Let alone; let us see whether Elias will come to take him down." Of course, the expression, 'Let alone,' in his lips, could not mean, Do not give him the vinegar. The word rendered 'Let alone' is one of those common phrases which people of all languages use when they are at work, to cheer, and rally, or check one another. We should say, "Hold on"; the Romans said, "Come on"; the Greeks said, "Let alone." Of course, the man himself would not have said, Let the vinegar alone, or, Let the sufferer alone, while he was in the act of giving him the vinegar. No; but while he gave it, he himself, in the exciting language of the moment, cries out, Come, or, Let alone; let us see whether Elias will come to take him down.

Is not this an inconsistency? that the man should have done an act of kindness to Christ, and at the same time have said this about Elias? How shall we explain it? He could not have been intelligently a friend of Christ. But it is certain that his act was a friendly act. No ill motive could have prompted this relief. We can make several suppositions with regard to the state of mind in which he performed this kindness, and all of them will suggest some instruction; for the friends of Christ are of all varieties, and their faith and their love is of every degree and shade.

When this man gave Christ the cooling drink, saying, at the same time, Let us see whether Elias will come to save him, I observe, —

I. The relenting crucifier may have wished to conceal his interest in Christ.

It is not uncommon for those who are really convinced upon the subject of religion, and deeply impressed, to use arts to conceal their feelings. Shame is one of the most powerful principles of the human mind. Not unfrequently, when an individual in a family, or company of friends, is strongly interested in religion, many devices are resorted to, in order that others may not discover or suspect him. For this purpose, some leave the house of God where they have been weeping under the exhibition of their condition and danger as sinners, and will immediately enter into conversation with others with more than usual interest and earnestness, upon ordinary topics, sometimes even of a jocose nature, to prevent suspicion of any unusual interest in religion. Having succeeded, they go to their places of retirement, and seek to renew the feelings which they had in the sanctuary. But, alas! they find those feelings deadened; they wonder that they cannot feel as they did within the hour. There is, however, no cause for wonder. They have grieved the Holy Spirit of God by whom they would have been sealed unto the day of redemption. They have been ashamed of Christ. They have denied him before men. They cannot reasonably hope that their feelings will be the same as they were, before they, by this unhappy means, grieved the Spirit.

Sometimes, in the company of those with whom religion is unpalatable, one is impelled to speak a serious word, or give a serious tone to the conversation, or involuntarily use a religious expression. Then, for fear that his friends will shout, or wink, he follows his accidental or impulsive expression with some slight levity, or sort of apology, to screen himself from ridicule. What hearts these are, to be ashamed of God, and of Christ; to blush at that which should be our glory, to cower and quake before those whom, perhaps, we shall one day hear calling on rocks and mountains to cover them, and, it may be, for some once-despised Lazarus to bring them a drop of water. Yet many do deny Christ in the presence of his enemies in this manner, even when they have a bias wholly in his favor, and, indeed, if left to themselves, do feel and express no little interest in religion. We may go further, and say, that some real follower of Christ may be so much overawed by opposition, or ridicule, or silent contempt, or by the presence of some whom he fears or respects, as to do that which, in his reflecting moments, will fill him with shame and pain. This was the case with Peter, who followed Christ afar off, and, being accused by a little maid before a company of just such men as we least like to encounter, — a company of idlers and loungers round a fire in a public place, — denied, with oaths and cursing, that he knew Christ. Yet Simon Peter was a friend of Christ, and went out and wept bitterly at having been ashamed of him.

But it may be that this man in the text, while he sought to practise concealment with regard to his feelings, acted only a prudent part. Wishing to do Christ a kind act, and yet knowing that any kindness to him would expose him to insult, and perhaps death; — with more reason than in any one of the cases which I have used as an illustration, perhaps he sought to conceal his interest in Christ, while he gave him a proof of his compassion. After all, there may have been nothing careless or wanton in his remark, "Let us see whether Elias will come to save him." When Christ said, "Eloi, Eloi," the resemblance of the word to the original of 'Elias' was such as to justify the mistake which the people made, saying, 'This man calleth for Elias.' The man in the text might innocently have supposed that Elias was expected to appear and rescue him, and so he may have used those words, which others were using, to cover an act of humanity, and not to expose his real feelings, which, in those circumstances, would have been to give that which is holy to the dogs. Without any stretch of charity, we may suppose that this was the state of the man's mind; for had he been exulting over Christ, and taunting him with 'Elias,' surely he would not have run to relieve the Saviour's thirst. He took some little time in doing it, making it a deliberate act. His arm is too short to reach the Saviour's lips; he snatches a stick from a boy in the crowd, or sees a tall stalk growing in the rocks of Golgotha, and breaks it off, and thrusts it into the sponge, and moistens the parched mouth of the sufferer; and while some might turn upon him and say, You are one of his friends, then — you begin to believe in the impostor — he hides his feelings, and prevents suspicion, by crying out, 'Let us see whether Elias will come to save him.' How natural is all this; the human heart is the same in all ages and in all circumstances. His concealment may not have been sinful; he effected his object, namely, to relieve Christ, and it may not have been his duty to say or do more or less than he did, from a prudent and justifiable regard for his own safety.

There is another supposition which is natural and instructive.

II. The relenting crucifier may have been a sincere inquirer.

He may have been a candid man, looking for evidence, deceived by others, and not having had opportunities for knowing the truth. Prejudiced against Christ by seeing him crucified, and in such company, he nevertheless would not join to insult him, but took opportunity to show him a kindness, saying, at the same time, He expects Elias; let us see if he will come. In such a case, he was a bold man, acting up to the degree of light which he enjoyed, and determined that the sufferer on the cross should not be further abused; but if he were innocent, and supernatural power would, therefore, soon befriend him, he was ready and willing to be convinced; in testimony of which, he slakes the thirst of Christ, as though he would do every thing to prolong life, till the question should be decided whether Elias would come. But whatever motive we ascribe to him, we are bound to believe, not only by that charity which hopeth all things, but by the nature of his act, which surely is not contradicted by his words, that he had feelings of kindness and compassion toward the Saviour.

As we contemplate this incident at the cross, several reflections are naturally suggested.

1. *Christ, on the cross for our sins, is reduced to such extremity that the most common act of humanity is grateful to him.*

And has it come to this — God manifest in the flesh! Is there, for thee, a depth of degradation so low, a depth of misery so great, that to sip the vinegar from a sponge is acceptable and comforting? O, wretched man that I am, to have brought Christ to this condition by my sins. For us he became obedient unto death, even the death of the cross, and with it submitted to all the humiliating circumstances of crucifixion. Yet how many have read and heard this, and have never said, It was for me; nor has it interested them to consider whether Christ received the vinegar or the wine, from a sponge or from a cup. Well does he say, "Is it nothing to you, all ye that pass by? Behold, and see if there be any sorrow like unto my sorrow." In sickness, we have ministering angels about us, in human shape, and there is nothing that ingenuity can invent, or love and kindness furnish, which does not abound toward us. But when the Saviour dies, it is upon the nails driven through his hands and feet; the thirst made by his intolerable anguish is served with a sponge full of vinegar; and all the spectators propose to wait and see whether Elias will come to help him. This is not related of one in whom we have no concern except as his fellow-creatures; all this was for each of us; "he was wounded for our transgressions, he was bruised for our iniquities." The recital of these sufferings on the part of Christ should move the soul of every man to say, What can I do, and what should I be, for Him who loved me, and gave himself for me? Nothing can be more reasonable than that every one who hears and believes such things as these should be a decided and earnest friend of his Redeemer.

2. *Christ will one day behold each of us in the same need of compassion and help in which we have now contemplated him.*

We see Christ suffering, in humiliation and pain beyond degree; we see him accepting the meanest offering, gratefully, to relieve his anguish.

The hour of nature's extremity is approaching to every one of us. Helpless, as infancy, we shall depend wholly upon other hearts and hands, and they will be ready, nay, too anxious, to comfort and serve us. But there is a help in that hour which friends cannot render. We shall forget the body and its pains in the thought of the soul and its vast concerns. In that hour, beloved friend, companion in tribulation, one thought of Christ as your compassionating Friend, will be to you inexpressibly precious. It can be secured by being now, while in health and strength, a friend of Christ. What if his sufferings never excited your compassion; you cannot expect that yours will excite his. If you never gave him the smallest testimony of your love, what can you expect from him? All these incidents of Christ's sufferings are recorded expressly to move our feelings, to bring Christ very near to us, by exciting us to sympathize with him; but, if our hearts are not moved, let us fear lest, when we, too, are dying, he who tasted the bitter cup for us will not feel that he can, consistently, bestow upon us his compassion, or, lest we feel ashamed or unwilling to ask an injured, neglected Saviour for his aid.

But there is another hour, more affecting even than the hour of sickness and dying — the hour when we shall see him face to face. There we shall think of his death for us; there, the minutest circumstances of his pain and shame will visit our thoughts. If they never led us to befriend him, we cannot look for any thing from him but neglect. And when he comes with clouds, and every eye shall see him, and they also that pierced him, and all kindreds of the earth shall wail because of him, and we, with his crucifiers, are at his bar, we shall be numbered with his unrelenting crucifiers, unless we have repented and accepted the offered Redeemer. They who drove the nails and spear into him were by no means sinners above all others. We, who have enjoyed such light, have 'pierced him' more, by our treatment of him, than they.

If this relenting crucifier really believed on Jesus, then or afterward, his kindness to the Saviour will be to him a source of recollection which the world could not purchase. So may we do something for Christ, for his cause, for his poor, afflicted saints, of which he will hereafter say, Ye did it unto me. But unless we love Christ, our motives are defective.

Let us stand, in imagination, at the cross. All those sufferings, that entire atoning sacrifice, are necessary to save one soul. We do not, we cannot, divide our interest in Christ with the race, nor with one of them; the whole sacrifice of the Redeemer is required for the justification of each sinner. It was necessary for Christ to become flesh, for Christ to die, in order to save your soul. If so, then each of us may say, I am the occasion of that cross. I brought the Saviour from heaven to the accursed tree.

Does this excite no contrite feeling within us? We see at the cross some who are befriending Christ; the beloved disciple and Mary Magdalene. Are we at heart with them? or does our interest in the sufferer not even rise so high as that of a relenting crucifier? One single emotion of love and gratitude to Christ, from you, will be as grateful to him as was that cooling draught to his lips. One look, with an eye of faith, upon the Son of man lifted up for you, would enable him to say for you, "It is finished;" and all the benefits of his death would, by one act of a believing, contrite heart, become yours.

But, while you hesitate, or pass carelessly by the cross, as though it were nothing to you, the time draws nigh, when, instead of his knocking at the door of our hearts, we shall knock at his door, and any delay to admit us will bring with it alarm and dismay. The Man of Calvary is now exalted to be a Prince and Saviour, to give repentance and remission of sins. Now is the time to ensure forgiveness and acceptance through his death, and to prove the sincerity of our love to him by deeds of kindness and affection toward him, his people, and his cause. No more will he come dependent upon a relenting crucifier for a slight act of mercy to refresh his dying lips; no more will it be at the option of sinners to accept or to reject him. "BEHOLD, HE COMETH WITH CLOUDS; AND EVERY EYE SHALL SEE HIM, AND THEY ALSO THAT PIERCED HIM; AND ALL KINDREDS OF THE EARTH SHALL WAIL BECAUSE OF HIM. EVEN SO. AMEN."

SERMON XII.

JOSEPH OF ARIMATHEA.

MATT. XXVII. 57, 58.

WHEN THE EVEN WAS COME, THERE CAME A RICH MAN OF ARIMATHEA, NAMED JOSEPH, WHO ALSO HIMSELF WAS JESUS' DISCIPLE. HE WENT TO PILATE, AND BEGGED THE BODY OF JESUS. THEN PILATE COMMANDED THE BODY TO BE DELIVERED.

AMONG the dark things of the ancient Scriptures to the mind of a pious Jew, no doubt this prophecy respecting the Messiah was mysterious and perplexing: "And he made his grave with the wicked, and with the rich in his death." A celebrated Jewish infidel rejected the prophecy of Isaiah chiefly on account of the remarkable coincidences between its prophetic descriptions of Christ's death and the actual circumstances of it, proving, as he contended, that a description so minutely exact, must have been written by an eye-witness.

The allusion, in this prophecy, to the death and burial of Christ, contains, seemingly, a contradiction; and there was, indeed, a strange contrast between his death and his burial. " He made his grave with the wicked." The word "grave" is here used in an extended sense for a place of death; the passage may, therefore, be paraphrased thus: He was joined both with the wicked, and with rich men, in his death and burial. Joseph of Arimathea was a rich man, and also an honorable councillor, a member of the great Jewish council, the sanhedrim. In burying Christ, he was assisted by another honorable man, a ruler, Nicodemus. "And there came also Nicodemus, which at the first came to Jesus by night, and brought a mixture of myrrh and aloes, about a hundred pound weight." We infer that he was rich.

Behold these eminent men fulfilling the prophecy of Isaiah. That dark passage is made clear, and the reason annexed to the prophecy is also explained. These two rich men and rulers knew that he was a good man, that "he had done no violence, neither was any deceit in his mouth." The burial of Christ by these two men of reputation, was a testimony that he was all that he claimed to be, and no impostor. These incidental proofs that the Christian religion is from God, were arranged by its great Author, to convince and persuade men.

There are three things which are placed in a strong light by this interesting transaction — the burial of the Saviour by Joseph, assisted by Nicodemus.

I. The burial of the Saviour by Joseph and his friend is an interesting illustration of faith.

Christ was numbered with the transgressors. In the opinion of the multitude, his character as an impostor was proved by his inability to deliver himself from his enemies. 'He saved others, himself he cannot save.' 'If he be the King of Israel, let him now come down from the cross, and we will believe on him.' 'If thou be the Son of God, come down from the cross.' Little did they think that he bore their insults in silence because he was, in that hour, while suspended on those nails, making atonement for their sins, as some of them, there is reason to hope, learned afterward, at the day of Pentecost, when, with an eye of faith, they looked on him whom they had pierced, and mourned, and were in bitterness for him, as a man is in bitterness for a first-born. Though Joseph belonged to the council which condemned Christ, it is said of him, "The same had not consented to the counsel and deed of them." He had accepted the evidence that Jesus was the Christ. The popular fury had not affected his faith. He knew whom he believed. The sight of his Saviour blindfolded, spit upon, arrayed in mock royalty, holding a reed for a sceptre, and finally bearing the accursed cross, then nailed to the tree, and more than all, crying, My God, my God, why hast thou forsaken me? did not shake the faith of this man. We wonder not that any disbelieved, but the wonder is that any maintained their confidence. Such was the confidence of Joseph in the Saviour that he went to Pilate and begged the body of Jesus for interment, which of course he would not have done, had he supposed that Christ was not all which he professed to be. It seems as though his faith had rather increased than lessened, amid the terrible events of that day; for it inspired him with a desire to manifest his attachment to his Lord and Master by honoring his body. It would have been sufficient, in the view of many, to have believed on Christ privately, to have been a Christian at home, and to have kept his opinions to himself. Joseph made a public profession of his faith. Before the whole people of the Jews, and in the presence of that Roman governor who delivered Christ to be crucified, and who tried to wash the stain of that guilt from his soul by washing his hands, he took the dishonored form of Jesus from the cross and buried it.

He stood before the Roman governor. Notice the manner of his address. It is said that he 'went in boldly unto Pilate'; but though inspired with this great moral courage, still, it is said, he "begged" the body of Jesus. He knew his place as a subject. He did not revile the heathen governor, nor in any way behave himself unseemly. Calm and dignified in his faith and confidence, he respectfully makes his request: Grant me the body of the man who has been crucified between the thieves. Surely this was the triumph of faith, and, like his divine Master, this Joseph, in the presence of Pontius Pilate, witnessed a good confession.

To be a Christian seems, perhaps, to some of us, as difficult and impossible as it would have been to some, at the crucifixion, to do what Joseph did, and which, in their view, was a great reproach to him. What would have induced a scribe or priest to give the Saviour a reputable burial? The answer is easy: Faith, like Joseph's. It was because Joseph believed, that he made this act of confession. The apostles, when they were charged not to speak any more in the Saviour's name, said, "We cannot but speak the things which we have seen and heard." So, when we believe with all the heart, we shall not be hindered by trifles or great difficulties from professing Christ. Any man among us, however far he may now be from religion, may soon be seen confessing his divine and crucified Redeemer. The grace of God can make any man so strong in faith that he will long to profess, before all on earth and all in heaven, as Joseph did, that he is not ashamed of Christ. If our desires and faith were greater, we might oftener see wonderful instances of conversion, and of consecration to Christ.

II. In the conduct of Joseph, we have an illustration of moral courage and decision of Christian character.

In the view of many, the Saviour was the greatest malefactor of the three who were hanging on the cross. But even if he were not a malefactor, he had been disgraced; for it is written, "Cursed is every one that hangeth on a tree." It exposed any man to the loss of reputation to favor one who was subjected to crucifixion. But we read of Joseph, "This man went in boldly unto Pilate, and begged the body of Jesus." It was the body of one whom that governor had delivered to the accursed death of the cross, and the request of Joseph was an implied reflection on the governor. At the next meeting of the sanhedrim, what might Joseph expect would be his reception by them? There is the man, they might say, who took the body of the impostor from the cross, and buried it in his own tomb. Every epithet which scorn and hatred could heap upon him, he might expect would be in requisition against him. What a sight must that have been when this honorable man went boldly to the cross with his servants, and took from it the body of Jesus. Overhead remained the inscription designed for insult and triumph: "This is Jesus of Nazareth, the King of the Jews." Beneath the cross, the rapacious soldiers were parting the garments of the Saviour, and for his vesture casting lots. Passing by, the infidel Jew was repeating aloud the assurance which he strove to maintain, notwithstanding the miraculous darkness and the earthquake: "He saved others, himself he cannot save." But still, in this bold and public manner, this friend of Jesus conveys away that form on which earth and hell had poured their contempt; and he bestows upon it an honorable and costly burial. Who does not entertain for such a man a feeling of the deepest respect and reverence?

Yet with all the light which eighteen centuries have accumulated around the name of Christ and his religion, there are many who are ashamed of Christ. One hinderance to their conversion and salvation is, they are not willing to have it known that they are seeking religion. The thought of having certain persons look at them with the reflection, He is anxious about his salvation, or, He has become a Christian, is more than they can bear. How do they appear by the side of Joseph of Arimathea, who, with all that was repugnant to the natural and social feelings, in the circumstances of the Saviour, not only espoused his cause, but cherished his dishonored body, and committed his reputation, for evil or for good report, to that Redeemer whom his associates had slain and hanged upon a tree?

The Saviour said, "Whosoever cometh not after me, and taketh not up his cross daily, cannot be my disciple." Is there no opportunity for cross-bearing in our situation in life? Do none of us ever meet with occasions for it? Are you not thrown in connection with some to whom your sentiments and practice are obnoxious, or to whom they would be, if you were to become a Christian? How do you bear being called a 'bigot,' or 'exclusive,' because you will not admit that all are safe, believe as they may, and because you will not countenance those who reject truths which, with you, are essential to salvation, nor join with them in acts of religious fellowship? It is easy to swim with the tide; but we must stem the flood. There is a cross for every one to bear who is consistently and ardently devoted to Christ, and the promotion of his cause. The greatest part of the trial which it occasions, if not the whole of it, is in taking it up; afterward, as the Saviour said, 'the yoke is easy, and the burden light.' We shall next see what it was which imparted moral courage, and made the cross so light a burden, to the rich man of Arimathea.

III. The conduct of Joseph is an illustration of the power which ardent love for Christ has in the life and conduct.

Here was the secret of his courage, the hiding of its power. He loved Christ; the Saviour's rejection and sufferings had raised the affections of this friend to their highest pitch; and he bestowed upon the dead body of his Redeemer the utmost proofs of love.

He had prepared for himself a family tomb. No member of his family had yet occupied it. As he prepared that sepulchre, no doubt he sometimes thought of the first interment which should be made there, and he asked himself, unwillingly, which member of his household would be the first occupant of that sacred place. Had any applied to him for leave to bury an entire stranger there, perhaps his feelings would have revolted at the request. He might have said to himself, It is my family tomb; far distant be the day when we shall follow one of our number to the spot; yet, until the place is hallowed in this mournful manner, I would keep it sealed. But now, behold, the first occupant of that tomb is taken from what we should call the scaffold, the gibbet; from between two thieves; amid the execrations of a great city; and in the face of contempt and scorn without measure.

The body is detached from the cross; that 'descent from the cross' is the subject of the masterpiece of Rubens; but Rubens, even, could not paint the beauty and love of that attachment which moved this friend of the Saviour in performing the offices of this interment.

Let us follow the bier. Few, very few, even of the

friends of Christ, are there. The women that followed him from Galilee, ministering unto him, are there. The rest have smitten their breasts and returned. The miraculous darkness, the earthquake, the rending of the rocks, and the rumor that the graves themselves are opening, have withdrawn the multitudes from the cross. Mary Magdalene, of course, is there, and the beloved John. The body is laid on the bier, and borne in silence to a neighboring garden. Was there ever such a funeral procession? The Prince of life is going to the tomb. The Son of God is tasting death for every man. Where are the thronged streets, the sea of people, the bands of hired mourners and of them that make a noise? where are the chariots of state, and of private opulence? where the train of nobles? where is Jerusalem? A more obscure and neglected burial seldom took place. But what more could be expected in the burial of a crucified man? Arrived at the tomb, the body is prepared for the long sleep of death, by the two men who had thus showed their love to Christ. "Then took they the body of Jesus, and wound it in linen clothes with the spices, as the manner of the Jews is to bury." Though their love seems to be made perfect, their knowledge, or else their faith, is deficient. They appear to be expecting that he is to sleep like other men in death. Very little impression seems to have been made upon any of the disciples, by the Saviour's promise that he would rise again at the third day. Ere we blame them, or even wonder at them, let us consider, that promises, full as explicit and plain, are, by us, in the hour of our sorest need, wholly disregarded, and frequently forgotten.

There, in the new tomb, where he had expected first of all to be laid himself, or to lay some object of his love, Joseph places the body of his Lord, who was crucified in weakness, and in whom none but an eye of faith and a heart which had felt the power of a Saviour's love could see, amid all his humiliation and ignominious wounds, the Son of God and Saviour of the world. Herein is love. Joseph has bestowed on his deceased Master the greatest proof of sincere affection. John took the Saviour's mother to his own family and home; Joseph took the Saviour's body to his own family tomb. What price would have purchased an interment for that body in the high priest's tomb, or in the tomb of any other member of the sanhedrim except Joseph? What makes the difference? Love. Love can do miracles; love regards not human opinion, numbers, influence; intent on its object, it sees no difficulties, feels no burden. It was such love for us that brought the Saviour from heaven, and carried him to the cross. It was love for his and our Saviour, by which Joseph prepared a place in his own new tomb for him whom we by our sins had crucified.

This act of Joseph and of Nicodemus, in connection with their previous history, illustrates another and an encouraging truth.

IV. THE GRACE OF GOD CAN PREVAIL OVER HINDERANCES TO FAITH AND CHRISTIAN ZEAL IN THE CHARACTERS AND CIRCUMSTANCES OF MEN.

Here we have two men performing an act which required more courage and decision than any thing connected with the trying duty of professing Christ before his enemies, and as much real affection. Now, who are these two men? John describes both of them in succession: 'And after this, Joseph of Arimathea, being a disciple of Jesus, (but secretly for fear of the Jews,) besought Pilate that he might take away the body of Jesus.' "And there came also Nicodemus, (which at the first came to Jesus by night,) and brought a mixture of myrrh and aloes, about a hundred pounds weight."

It is certainly remarkable that the two men who performed this courageous act were men who once were exceedingly cautious, reserved, prudent, and, it may be, timid: — we cannot assert this; — but certainly they were careful and slow in their profession of faith in the Saviour. We do not find Peter here — that dear friend and ardent man, who said, "Though all men forsake thee, yet will not I." Where is Peter? Good at heart, but like his own lake of Galilee, subject to sudden and violent gusts of feeling, — Where is Peter? Perhaps he is finishing his repentance at his fall, while two men, who at first would not own themselves the disciples of Christ, are taking down His body from the accursed tree, and putting it into the tomb. God can place us in circumstances where our faith, though now like a bruised reed, shall suddenly acquire the strength of years, and as Joseph and Nicodemus, no doubt, wondered at themselves, and may have said, Can it be that we, once so reserved, are the only men in Jerusalem that dare to bury Jesus? so we, if we walk according to the light already given, may be permitted to perform acts of love for the Saviour which will fill us with wonder and joy. We naturally love to have men declare themselves on the side of Christ at once; and it is desirable that they should do so. John is an example of this — John, who was to his Lord and Master like the morning star, which glows in the sunrising, and in subsequent months shines as brightly in the west, the beautiful witness, still, of the monarch of the day when lost from our sight. Some are like John, bold and constant, from first to last; while others are slow and cautious. We must make allowance for the differences in natural disposition and temperament. Let us not despise the day of small things with regard to those who are backward, when thcy seem to have true grace; but let them increase in love to Christ, and love will, to them, be like a flood tide to a stranded ship, lifting and bearing them over every obstacle. Love Christ, and though you may have come to him, at first, "by night," the noonday will not be too bright, at last, to illustrate the full power of your attachment to him in acts of devotion.

V. The reward which Joseph had for his conduct, is an instance of the blessedness of those who love and serve Christ.

In two days, Joseph's tomb became the scene of an event, second to the scene on Calvary, only in the order of time. There, in that tomb, life and immortality were brought to light. Never had man a house or palace so honored as Joseph's tomb. It was occupied, first, by the lifeless form of the Son of God. Who may fully imagine what transpired there, as that form came to life again; what angelic ministrations were there; and what presence of glorified souls, to witness in the Saviour's resurrection the type and earnest of their own. "And behold, there was a great earthquake; for the angel of the Lord descended from heaven, and rolled back the stone from the door, and sat upon it. His countenance was like lightning, and his raiment white as snow; and for fear of him the keepers did shake, and became as dead men."

In progress of time, other guards and warriors have encircled Joseph's tomb. The armies of Europe and Asia have done battle for it; the wars of the crusaders were waged to rescue that same tomb from the infidels. To Joseph and his household, what associations must have been connected with that family tomb; and with what peace must he and they have buried their dead, to sleep in the Saviour's own bed of death. All the church of God thank and love thee, Joseph, for thy love and services to their Lord. They who give burial to a friend of ours that dies on a foreign shore, receive our thanks. He who took our Saviour from his cross, and laid him in his own new tomb, is a benefactor to the church of God. Forever, in the history of redemption, Joseph will be remembered in connection with his Saviour's death. As he bows in heaven at those sacred feet, he remembers that he once composed those bleeding feet, those bleeding hands, that bleeding head, for burial. At the last day, when, Judge of the world, Jesus shall sit with the nations at his bar, Joseph will remember, I laid him once in my own new tomb.

If, then, we wish for enduring honor and happiness, we must connect our names and influence with Christ and his cause. To be the builder and owner of all the pyramids, mausoleums, and obelisks of Egypt, and have your names and deeds emblazoned there, is not to be compared with being Joseph of

Arimathea, and the owner of that tomb. It is as true with regard to the most desirable reputation, as it is with regard to salvation, that other foundation can no man lay than that is laid, which is Jesus Christ. If you have influence to exert, it will, at last, be comparatively or wholly lost, unless it is in some way connected with his cause. If you have riches, you will perish with them, unless you and they are connected with the Saviour. If you have talents and genius, you will come to nought, unless they are consecrated to Christ and his kingdom. The greatest earthly statesmen, compared with angelic greatness, or with many of the spirits of just men made perfect, would be unnoticed, like lamps, or watch fires, left burning after the sun is high.

Every one of us has his own peculiar opportunity of showing to Christ his attachment to him. Joseph had his; that act of love was his profession of faith and piety. There is something for each of us to do, to test and show our love for Christ. It may not be published; but Christ, who sees in secret, will know it, and that will be sufficient reward. It is, therefore, a great mistake to think of religion only as we think of a shroud — an accompaniment of death. Lost time is most to be deplored for the loss of opportunities to serve and honor Christ.

While you have been considering this narrative, perhaps your love has been awakened toward Joseph for his conduct. Do you love Joseph for taking that body from the cross, and laying it in his own tomb? The Redeemer himself gave up that body to the cross for you; he went to the tomb for you; will you love the friend of Christ, and not love your infinite Friend? Your sensibilities can be moved by the tale of generous love and attachment in a fellow-creature; have you no emotion and no tears at the thought of Him who endured such grief, and bore such shame, and drank that bitter cup, and went from the ignominious cross to the sepulchre for you? Joseph begged the body of Jesus of the Roman governor. Jesus, when your soul and body were captives to Satan, encountered Satan, with agony unknown, and rescued you; "and having spoiled principalities and powers, he made a show of them openly, triumphing over them in it."

The door of the tomb will soon open, or a new-made grave wait, for you. But faith in Christ and love toward him will enable you to say, as David in spirit said on behalf of his Lord and Saviour, "My flesh also shall rest in hope." Your dust will then be the object of love and care to Christ, far more than his body was to the rich man of Arimathea; and at length you shall follow him from the sleep of the grave into life everlasting. "FOR IF WE HAVE BEEN PLANTED TOGETHER IN THE LIKENESS OF HIS DEATH, WE SHALL BE ALSO IN THE LIKENESS OF HIS RESURRECTION."

SERMON XIII.

THE WOMEN AT THE SEPULCHRE.

MATT. XXVII. 61.

AND THERE WAS MARY MAGDALENE, AND THE OTHER MARY, SITTING OVER AGAINST THE SEPULCHRE.

JOSEPH and his companions had rolled a great stone to the door of the sepulchre, and had departed. The silence of death and the grave had succeeded to the excitement of the crucifixion; the disciples were 'scattered every one to his own,' and left their Master in the narrow house. Two women, however, could not leave the spot. Enchained there as by a spell or trance, they sat down in the garden, when others had left the place, and gave themselves up to the luxury of grief. "And there was Mary Magdalene, and the other Mary, sitting over against the sepulchre."

"The other Mary," here mentioned, was the mother of James, and Judas, (not Iscariot,) and Joses, and, some say, Simon Zelotes. Two, if not three, of her sons were of the twelve apostles Happy mother!

By what methods of pious faithfulness and a godly life did so many of thy sons become such men that Jesus honored them with so great a distinction? Thou art called simply "the other Mary." But what a mother she must have been. We should expect that such a mother would love Christ ardently; and here we find her, while a great stone is rolled between her and the burying-place of her Redeemer, sitting over against it, as the dearest spot on earth in her affections.

Her companion is Mary Magdalene, a name to which, in the opinion of many judicious critics, injustice has unintentionally been done, partly through the inadvertence of readers of the Bible. Asylums for once depraved but penitent women are distinguished by her name, as though she were at the head of this class of sinners and penitents. But some insist that there is not a word in the Bible to show that she herself was a depraved woman. She is named in honorable connection with Joanna, the wife of Chuza, Herod's steward, who, it is thought, would not have subjected herself, being the wife of a high officer under government, to an association with such a woman as many suppose Mary Magdalene to have been. That seven devils had had possession of her, it is said, is no sufficient proof of her loose character. We are reminded that children were subject to demoniacal possession, and Mary's good standing and influence in society would, perhaps, have been as likely as any thing to attract the notice and excite the malignity of the devil and his angels. 'Magdalene' is derived from the name of the town, Magdala. There is not the least reason to suppose that she was the "woman that was a sinner," who wept at Jesus' feet, and who, without any authority for it, is generally called "Mary."

If she were immoral, still it is not necessary to suppose that she was a common, low character; we need not impute to her all that was vulgar and infamous in debauchery. Her continual association, however, in the minds of many, with persons of such a stamp, awakens in others a disposition to vindicate her even from every kindred imputation.

But while she may have been a woman of rank and influence, no one can positively assert that she was not a courtesan, — a select and private transgressor, preëminent in her arts and in mischief. Yet, in the absence of a word of proof to this effect, our feelings naturally incline us to hope better things. Whether she had been a great sinner or not, she had been a great sufferer. Seven devils had made her their prey. The gates of hell had almost prevailed against her, when the mighty Conqueror, Jesus, had plucked her out of their hands. No one had more to be grateful for than she; and well might she linger at the tomb of her infinite Friend, to her the dearest spot on earth. Will those fiends assail her again, now that Jesus is dead? Has hell triumphed? What a loss to her, apparently, is the death of Christ. To whom shall she go but unto him?

Approaching night at last compelled these women to leave the tomb. But when they left the sepulchre, it was on an errand of love to Christ. "And they returned, and prepared spices and ointments." Joseph and Nicodemus had wrapped the body in a hundred pounds of dry spices, such as myrrh and aloes, by which the bleeding wounds were stanched, and the body would seem to be kept for some time in a state of preservation. The women had no intention, of course, of embalming the body, properly speaking; but they meant to anoint the face, and hands, and feet, with fragrant oils and balm, with just the feeling with which we strew flowers around the dead. To embalm the body was not the work of women. Their purpose was the beautiful suggestion of love and honor, to bestow some expression of care and affection upon the precious remains.

"And they returned, and prepared spices and ointments" that same night; and the very next morning, by daybreak, we may expect that they will visit the tomb, and execute their purpose. But no; they waited one whole day. Why is this? Is their love so suddenly grown cold? "They rested the Sabbath day, according to the commandment."

What pious reverence for the day of God do we find here. Even the desire to bestow honor upon Jesus does not lead these women to visit his tomb on the Sabbath. Christ was the Lord of the Sabbath. Will not this give them permission to leave their place of worship? They will think of nothing but the sepulchre, if they go to public worship; and may they not properly go where their hearts are? Can they serve God better than by showing respect to the body of his Son? Thus many would reason for them, and excuse them. We respect, we reverence them, for this powerful example of regard for the day of holy rest. It is a gentle and kind admonition to those who visit cemeteries on the Sabbath, to weep at the graves of kindred. Jesus was left alone in his tomb on the Sabbath; a Sabbath which then commemorated only the creation of the world. We should not prize and honor our Christian Sabbath, with its more precious associations, less. Our regard for holy time should restrain us from doing that which the piety of these Jewesses would not do even for the Saviour of the world.

And was it any real deprivation and loss to those women that they could not visit the sepulchre on the Sabbath? In their secret places, and in the house of God, separated from the object that would move their sensibilities to no good purpose, they spent a far more profitable day than by 'sitting over against the sepulchre.' There, the dead body of Christ would engage their thoughts; but at home, in communion with God, who is a Spirit, to whom they owed a duty superior to their regard for the mortal part even of Jesus, they could worship their Maker in spirit and in truth. Though they had known Christ after the flesh, yet, for that day, they would know even him, in that respect, no more.

Such a Sabbath was never beheld before or since. The Prince of Life was in the grave; the Word that was made flesh had left his body in the sepulchre; the earth, in that one revolution on its axis, bore a strange freight, a priceless treasure, in its bosom. 'The Resurrection and the Life' is sleeping the short sleep of death. The almighty Saviour has with him, in that tomb, our hopes, and our heaven, and the keys of death and hell. What if ensuing weeks should still behold the Saviour in the tomb. It is easy to see why all who love Christ cherish the day when he arose. They do not need laws and prohibitions to give them that superior relish for the sacred pleasures of the Lord's day which makes the world and its pleasures distasteful. There is enough in the sacred recollections suggested by the Lord's day to fill up the hours with profitable thoughts and duties, if we have the feelings of true believers in Christ. Then, we have no need to ask concerning any amusement or business, Is it lawful to do this on the Sabbath day? A heart that is right with God is a sound casuist.

It was "yet dark" on the first day of the week when these women came to the sepulchre. It was an interesting, a touching instance of that presumption to which love is prone, that these women should have gone to that place with the purpose for which they had prepared themselves. There was a guard around the tomb. Would that guard suffer Christ's disciples to have access to his body? Surely not. Suppose that they would; how were these women to roll that stone away? They said to themselves, as though they had just thought of it, "Who shall roll us away the stone from the door of the sepulchre?" This is a beautiful instance of womanly forgetfulness of difficulty, in pursuit of a favorite object. Woman will go close up to a mighty stone between herself and the object of her enterprising love, with no prospect of its being removed, yet borne on by something which can hardly be called hope, it being more like presumption; when man would foresee all the difficulties, and more prudently avoid them. But it is interesting to see how God oftentimes appears, and rolls away great stones for those who, with faith and love, march boldly on to the utmost limit of seeming possibility. Had we this simple love and courage, we might say to many a thing that obstructs our path, 'Who art thou, O great mountain? thou shalt become a plain.'

("And when they looked, they saw that the stone was rolled away;) for it was very great." The words following the parenthesis, give the reason why they asked among themselves for help. But some one had been there before them. "And behold, there was a great earthquake; for the angel of the Lord descended from heaven and rolled back the stone from the door, and sat upon it. His countenance was like lightning, and his raiment white as snow; and for fear of him the keepers did shake, and became as dead men."

And did this heavenly being, able thus to strike terror into those Roman soldiers by his presence, sit quietly in heaven, while that Saviour was in the hands of his enemies, and they were nailing him to the cross? Has he not come too late? Why not interpose at the cross, instead of the tomb? How easy it would have been for this bright seraph to have routed that host of crucifiers, priests and scribes, and soldiers, by appearing to them in his heavenly glory. Twelve legions of them, too, would have had their hands upon their swords, at one word of Christ. But how would the Scriptures have been fulfilled, that thus it must be? What means this forbearance, and why did Christ thus patiently suffer? For you, O my soul, for you, angels stand aloof, till men had 'killed the Prince of Life'; 'that he by the grace of God should taste death for every man.' It is finished! the day of triumph has arrived; now we shall see all heaven, "the helmed cherubim and sworded seraphim," around the tomb. It is not so. What economy of strength, what forbearance from needless display. One angel is commissioned to do this work of preparing for the Saviour's resurrection. Christ, by his own word, could have rolled the stone away; but it is deemed proper that one of his servants shall do it for him. Happy, honored spirit, to be selected for such a work. Worlds of treasure, ages of bliss, for that privilege, to unseal that stone, to look in and see the Resurrection and the Life revive!

There is something remarkable and instructive here. Christ was crucified publicly, and all who wished, might exult, and reject him, and insult over him. He rises from the dead, as he promised, on the third day, but he rises in secret. No mortal eye beholds that triumph. Why was not his resurrection as public as his crucifixion? Why was not Jerusalem, or the sanhedrim at least, gathered round his tomb, to see his triumph? What an opportunity to convince and convert them. They could not pretend that he was not dead, and that the sleep of the grave had revived him. The blood and water following the soldier's spear, every anatomist among them knew, was proof positive of death; but before that, the soldiers had forborne to break his legs, because they saw that he was dead. Now, to see that great stone roll away before the single-handed effort of a crucified man, alone within the tomb, and his coming out to life and strength before his enemies, would have struck them with confusion; it would have established his claims forever as the Christ. Why was it not so? Why crucified in public, and raised without one mortal eye to witness the resurrection? and after he was risen, seen only by companies of his friends? enough, indeed, to establish his resurrection beyond reasonable dispute, and yet in so private a manner, when a public demonstration could have confuted every gainsayer?

Thus God deals with men while on probation. He is never lavish with his proof; he will never over-persuade; but we are free agents; and this, we may truly say, is the great characteristic of the government of God: it is based on our being free, and not machines; or, in other words, we are governed by motives, and not by force.

In pursuance of the great plan of governing men, God, in his infinite majesty, refuses to afford his enemies more evidence than he sees to be suitable for their conviction. Christ spake in parables for this same reason, that they who were disposed to learn might inquire further, and they who were disposed to cavil might be offended, if they chose to be, at the appearance of difficulty which the parable gave to the truth. It required attention and thought to search out the meaning of the parable; which was plain, or would be made so, to the humble inquirer, while the unbeliever was repulsed by the appearance of mystery.

There is something sublime and deeply impressive in this feature of God's dealings with men. The doctrines of the gospel are so plainly revealed, that the humblest mind can find them on the surface; but the proud and self-sufficient reasoner, with all his books before him, cannot find that which is perfectly obvious to the 'dairyman's daughter,' and the 'shepherd of Salisbury Plain.' We cannot fail to reverence that reserve in the divine sovereignty which forbore to make the resurrection of Christ as public as his crucifixion. The great thing for man to do, is, to believe; but, to cultivate faith, there must not be too much sight. So that, if we are in any degree sceptical with regard to the evidences of religion, we must remember that if God had made the subject any plainer, it might have been to our spiritual injury; at the same time, all who are disposed to believe, find sufficient, and more than sufficient, evidence to support their faith.

The angel that terrified the guard spoke kindly to the women, and assured them that Christ had risen; and he sent them to the disciples with the news. "They fled from the sepulchre with fear and great joy, and ran to bring his disciples word. And their words seemed to them like idle tales, and they believed them not."

And yet how often Christ had told these disciples, saying, The Son of man shall be crucified, and the third day he shall rise again. When the people asked him for a sign, he said that no sign should be given them but that of Jonas the prophet. For as Jonah was three days and three nights in the whale's belly, so shall the Son of man be three days and three nights in the heart of the earth. Still, when the news came that all this was done as Christ had foretold them, they believed not.

Not wholly unlike this incredulity, this unbelief of theirs, is that which we mourn over in ourselves. How slow of heart we are to believe the Scriptures, the promises and the threatenings. How little effect the descriptions of the last judgment, and of heaven and hell, have upon us. Let us be reproved by these disciples, whom Christ afterward upbraided because they believed not them which had seen him after that he was risen.

John and Peter ran together to the sepulchre. John outran Peter, and reached the place before him, yet went he not in. He tells us himself that he went not in. This is not strange, in such a man as John. His feelings were too deep, too powerful, to allow him to enter that place. Suppose that the body of Christ were there; he shrunk from the sight of his Master sleeping in the grave. Suppose that he were not there; the shock which the certainty that he had risen would give him, he dreaded; he lingered a while, prolonging the painful pleasure of uncertainty. Peter soon arrives, and with the characteristic boldness with which he twice threw himself into the sea to meet Christ, he goes directly into the tomb. 'Then went in also that other disciple which came first to the sepulchre, and he saw and believed.'

Some of the minute incidents of Scripture are of great importance, and whatever is thought worthy of being recorded by the pen of inspiration we ought not to overlook. An illustration of this is the account which is given of the manner in which the grave clothes were found in the tomb. Peter 'seeth the linen clothes lie, and the napkin that was about his head not lying with the grave clothes, but wrapped together in a place by itself. Of what importance are these two incidents? They are of very great importance; they are circumstantial proof that the body of Christ was not stolen away, either by the hand of affection or by rapine, by friends or foes. Had friends carried the body away, it would have been unnatural, and without any assignable reason, that they should not have taken it in its wrappings. Had enemies taken it, the linen cloth and the spices in it were more valuable than the dead body, and too valuable to leave behind. Besides, there is design, deliberation, care, manifest in the disposition of these clothes. Thieves would not have wrapped together that napkin so carefully, and laid it in a place by itself. Some hand has been at work here which had no need of haste.

There is an air of truth about this whole narrative; for, instead of reading that all the disciples were convinced beyond a doubt that Christ was risen, and calling upon all men to believe it without wavering, we are told that Peter went away from the sepulchre, and from the circumstantial evidence there of Christ's resurrection, wondering in himself at that which had come to pass. We may appeal to any doubting mind, Was it an impostor who wrote this? An impostor would have shunned to let you see his lingering doubts; his great reluctance to believe; the weakness of his faith. He would have been full of assurance and demonstration, and would have demanded your belief, like a highwayman; but these apostles tell us that they themselves, at first, did not believe, and that it took very much to convince them. What a book, we say again, is the Bible, not only in its subjects, but in the methods by which it kindly gains credit for itself with the human understanding. What candor, simplicity, perfect transparency, in these writers; men who afterward, in attestation of the gospel, sealed their record with their blood. Who, after reading some of these incidents of the resurrection and of the apostles' feelings and conduct, and their own simple-hearted account of things, can doubt that they are honest and true? If honest and true, all they say is true; if so, the New Testament is true; if the New Testament is true, the Old Testament, which Christ fully confirmed, is true also; and if the Bible is true, we must receive it as the word of God, with all its mysteries and doctrines.

These wondering disciples left the empty sepulchre and went home. But Mary Magdalene stood without at the sepulchre weeping. What can she want more? That spot was the last at which she saw Jesus, and she cannot, will not, leave it. Peter and John have told her that it is empty, and told her, also, how they found the clothes lying. Why does she not go home with them? Infatuation of love! She will stay at that empty and forsaken place, and weep. But see her strange behavior. "And as she wept, she stooped down, and looked into the sepulchre." What can she look for? Will she believe even her own senses, if she does not believe the angel and the two disciples? Probably not; she is in a maze of grief; she loves Christ with an intenseness of love which seems to have no parallel. He delivered her out of the hand of the devil; if she never finds him again, she will never more find peace; and so, with an unsatisfied, restless feeling, she stoops down, and looks into the vacant and dark tomb.

But O, there is something there to see — two angels in white, sitting, the one at the head, and the other at the feet, where the body of Jesus had lain. They did not appear to Peter and John, but they were doubtless there. Angels have the power of making themselves visible or invisible in a moment. They did not appear to these apostles; they were not in a frame of mind to be rewarded by such a heavenly favor. But this weeping woman sought Christ with a hope which nothing could subdue. Like the ship, which makes the sure and steadfast anchor hold its place the more that the adverse wind urges her away from it, this mourner felt herself moored to the spot where every thing that she saw only made her weep. Such a sight as this was a recompense for all her constancy of love. As in the holy of holies the two cherubim stood over the ark of the covenant, looking at each other, so over the place where the body of Jesus had lain, these two angels sat, face to face. Ye heavenly spirits! why should that place be so dear to you? What is the grave to you? Why watch upon the ground where Jesus lay, when he has departed? 'These things angels desire to look into.' It was their God incarnate, as well as our Saviour. That tomb was the place where the gospel received its last confirmation;

every miracle, every word of Christ, every claim, every promise, every threatening, would have gone for nothing with men, had he failed to rise from the dead. There he was declared 'to be the Son of God with power.' Those angels might have sat there to this day, and never yet have exhausted the theme of wonder and joy suggested by that spot. It is a place for our thoughts to visit with the deepest interest every Sabbath morning, as soon as we regain our consciousness, and think, This is the Lord's day. O, what a day to the Christian is the Sabbath. He does not need Sinai to thunder it in his ears: — "Remember the Sabbath day to keep it holy."

Woman, why weepest thou? said these heavenly friends. So may it be said to us, as often as we look down into a sepulchre of a dear friend, or the place of our own expected burial, if we belong to Christ. Why weepest thou? As soon as she had replied, They have taken away my Lord, and I know not where they have laid him, she turned suddenly, perhaps at the sound of a step, and saw Jesus standing, and knew not that it was Jesus. Jesus said to her, Woman, why weepest thou? She thought him to be the gardener. With a respectful salutation she addresses that servant, who, she supposes, may have removed the body of her injured and despised Lord. Could he have been offended at having the crucified one in his master's new tomb? Sir, if thou have borne him hence, tell me where thou hast laid him, and I will take him away.

Jesus saith unto her, Mary! She turned herself; for she had spoken to the supposed gardener without looking at him. She turned herself, and saith unto him, Rabboni! Master! Jesus saith unto her, Touch me not; that is, Do not stay to manifest your love to me, for I am not immediately to ascend to my Father; but go to my brethren, and say to them, I ascend to my Father, and to your Father, to my God, and to your God.

Having fulfilled this errand, Mary Magdalene, with the other Mary, falls into the company of believers and friends, undistinguished by any further mention of them, till, at last, they rise, one after another, to meet that Saviour face to face, and to enjoy in heaven the fulness of that love, of which the foretaste here was heaven upon earth.

And what must heaven be to Mary Magdalene, delivered from such a bondage to Satan, and made one of the principal friends of Christ. Can we suppose that after such intimate love between her and her Saviour, he, in his kingdom, keeps her at a distance, and looks at her and speaks to her with royal dignity, and the cold propriety of earthly courts? He prayed that his friends might be with him, to behold his glory. We must believe that among that redeemed company, there is no one who loves Christ with more fervor and joy than Mary Magdalene. Her probable happiness in her intimacy with Christ, in heaven, shows what we shall enjoy, if, like her, we have "loved much."

We might all vie with her in heaven, had we as much to be grateful for to Christ as she,—had Christ done as much for us, as for her.

Has not Christ done as much, personally, for some of us? Has he not delivered us not merely from seven devils, indeed, but from the devil and his angels? When you see Satan and his angels doomed to fire, and lost men doomed with them, and going to be their prey, which of you would suffer Mary Magdalene to say that she owes more to Christ than you? If we but saw and felt our ruined condition, the evil of sin, and our fearful danger, we should, even here, love Christ as Mary loved him. What might not some of us have been, had we not been converted? Our hardened hearts, and stubborn wills, and depraved passions, and our fearful transgressions, might have been more dreadful than to have had seven evil spirits, as Mary had. Yes, each of us owes, or will owe, to Christ as large a debt of gratitude as she. We shall be forever paying it at his feet, and in his blissful service, or, for neglecting to love such a Saviour, 'depart,' accursed by Christ.

Those friends of Christ whom, in these discourses

we have contemplated, and of whom, as a class, we now take our leave, have witnessed to us, in every condition and age of life, that Christ is worthy to be believed, and to be loved; that he deserves all the heart, and soul, and mind, and strength.

The wise men have travelled in our sight from the distant east, to worship Christ. Aged Simeon has held him forth to us in his arms. John the Baptist, than whom there is no greater among men, has rejoiced to perceive the light of his glory become pale before his Emmanuel and ours. The wedded pair at Cana have spoken to the young that they remember Christ in the season of their espousals. The twelve apostles of the Lamb present their names to us in the foundations of the new Jerusalem, as witnesses for Jesus. The children in the temple have called upon children every where to sing hosannas to the Son of David. A woman that was a sinner presses by you to the Saviour's feet, her repentance and her love contending for the mastery. Martha has turned at his rebuke, from being careful and troubled about many things, and has joined her sister, at Jesus' feet, in choosing the good part which shall never be taken away from her. Simon the Cyrenian, that African, staggering under the ignominious cross which he bore for his Saviour, has said to you, Let us go forth therefore unto him without the camp, bearing his reproach. The penitent thief has reproved the unbelief of every, even the greatest, sinner, and has gone with Christ from the cross to a more than earthly paradise. The relenting crucifier has rebuked those who, familiar with the Saviour's sufferings, are crucifying him afresh. Joseph of Arimathea, once a secret disciple of Christ, and Nicodemus, who also came to Jesus by night, have instructed those who are intellectual and cautious, how to be bold, and to confess Christ before men. Once more, that love to Christ, which is stronger than death, is represented to us again in those women sitting over against his sepulchre and manifesting an ardor of love, which many waters could not quench, nor floods drown.

Our feelings and our lives may be such that, in heaven, when angels speak of the friends of Christ on earth, honorable mention can be made of us as the sincere and ardent, though it may be, as in some of these instances before us, humble, friends of the Redeemer.

Friend or enemy, each of us soon will meet Christ. Life, then, as a season of preparation for eternity, life, in all its precious privileges and opportunities, will seem to have been of infinite value. That life we enjoy to-day; and this day we may repent, believe, and have a friendship formed between ourselves and Christ, the history of which, on earth and in heaven, may be such as to make angels lean upon their harps, to learn new wonders in redeeming love

By his manger, his infancy, his interest in our happiness, his efforts for our good in his life; by his betrayal, and sufferings, and death; by his cross and by his tomb; by his resurrection and by his second coming, he invites us to be his friends. Jesus, the Saviour, should never be left to ask a second time for our friendship. His friends are multiplying. His cause is advancing, till it shall fill the earth. No one of us professes to be among his enemies; yet this is his own decision: "He that is not for me is against me, and he that gathereth not with me scattereth abroad." Many are leaving you for the service and the kingdom of Christ; will you forego the privileges and blessedness of being his friend?

Beloved brethren in Christ, these words, which may appropriately close these histories and appeals, are addressed by the Saviour himself to all, in every age, like you: "YE ARE MY FRIENDS, IF YE DO WHATSOEVER I COMMAND YOU. HENCEFORTH, I CALL YOU NOT SERVANTS; FOR THE SERVANT KNOWETH NOT WHAT HIS LORD DOETH; BUT I HAVE CALLED YOU FRIENDS."

THE FRIENDS OF CHRIST
IN THE NEW TESTAMENT:
THIRTEEN DISCOURSES;
By NEHEMIAH ADAMS, D. D.,
PASTOR OF THE ESSEX STREET CHURCH, BOSTON.

FIFTH EDITION.

JOHN P. JEWETT, AND COMPANY, . . . 117 Washington Street.

Price, One Dollar. pp. 295.

The object of this book is to illustrate faith in Christ, and love towards him, by the examples of those who befriended him when he was on earth.

CONTENTS. — 1. The Wise Men from the East; 2. Simeon; 3. John the Baptist; 4. The Bridegroom and Bride at Cana; 5. The Twelve Apostles; 6. The Children in the Temple; 7. The Woman with the Alabaster Box; 8. Martha and Mary; 9. Simon the Cyrenian; 10. The Penitent Thief; 11. The Relenting Crucifier; 12. Joseph of Arimathea; 13. The Women at the Sepulchre.

OPINIONS OF THE PRESS.

Puritan Recorder, Boston.

A rare combination of various learning, forcible reasoning, graceful diction, felicitous illustration, beautiful simplicity, and pertinent application.

Boston Traveller.

Every way worthy of the fine taste, superior scholarship, and unaffected Christian spirit of the author.

Boston Christian Watchman and Reflector, (Baptist.)

The volume belongs among the best.

Christian Witness, (Episcopal.)

They will be read with pleasure and profit.

Zion's Herald, (Methodist.)

Conceived in a delightful spirit, and written with rare ability both of thought and style.

Boston Congregationalist.

Those who neglect to place this volume upon one of the selectest shelves of their library will miss doing justice to the most original, most affluent, and most useful volume of sermons which the American press — at least for a long time — has given to the world.

Notice of the second edition, from the same.

It is a volume that will live, and not die, and as long as it lives will nourish and develop the germs of piety. The portraitures of Christian character are so accurate and finely wrought, lifelike and natural in their conception and finish, that they thrill the soul continually.

Boston Christian Examiner, (Unitarian.)

We have received from it edification and instruction of the most precious kind. . . . We have noticed many admirable features in this volume, expressing some noble truths in chaste and eloquent language. . . . The earnest and devoted zeal of the Christian minister to commend the character and offices of the Saviour to the love and faith of human hearts is apparent in the whole volume.

Boston Daily Advertiser.

These Sermons were listened to with great interest when delivered, and the following opinion of them, from a distant country, will, we doubt not, be responded to by many: —

Extract of a letter from Rev. James Hamilton, D. D., London, to a gentleman in Boston, February 8, 1853.

"Many thanks do I owe you for your valuable present of Dr. Adams's Discourses. They are at once so sound and so fresh, so solid and so lively, so full of instruction and so practical, that I am sure they will be very popular and useful. Even outwardly it is a noble book. A London publisher, to whom I showed it, was quite struck with its beautiful typography."

New York Evangelist.

The beauty of style, tenderness of feeling, and richness of doctrinal and experimental truth which the Discourses display, are of high order. Some of the portraitures of character are exquisite, and the hand of the artist is visible in all.

New York Journal of Commerce.

They enrich and adorn our Christian literature. We have to ascribe it to the fine creative talent of the preacher that these examples of faith and love toward Christ are reproduced in the full power of their actual life and beauty.

New York Observer.

Greatly refreshed and strengthened have we been by the perusal of these Sermons. Fragrant with the gentle spirit of the gospel, they are eminently fitted to mould and improve the character, while they inspire the earnest sentiments of devotion in the heart.

New York Independent.

This beautiful volume will become a favorite in very many Christian families. We can suggest no book more appropriate than this to those who would supply themselves with a choice and fragrant alabaster box of religious instruction, or who would give such to their friends.

Portland Christian Mirror.

A happy conception, this series of Discourses, and as happily executed. Without affectation or bluster, they quietly find their way to the conscience and the heart. You find within you meltings of spirit, yearnings of heart. without any forewarnings of such effects. It is a precious family book; a treasure to any member of the family of Christ.

New York Correspondent of Puritan Recorder.

Through the kindness of a friend in Boston, your correspondent has enjoyed the privilege of reading the "Friends of Christ in the New Testament." A book so rich in evangelical truth, so full of graphic descriptions of Scripture scenes, and so admirable in its tone of Christian feeling, must be, sooner or later, widely read.

Philadelphia Christian Observer.

A beautiful book in every respect — able, rich in thought, eloquent in the best sense of the term, commending the truth in holy beauty. Those who dare not encounter the reading of a volume of sermons will not be likely to lay this book aside unread.

Western Christian Advocate, (Cincinnati, O.)

The work is possessed of superior merit.

Bibliotheca Sacra, (Andover.)

These themes have the charm of novelty. They are treated with an originality, an unction, an inwardness of spirit, which in these days of commonplace and outwardness make one's soul to come again.